The
Tropical
Forest

The Tropical Forest

Ants, Ants, Animals & Plants

BY MARY BATTEN

Illustrated by Betty Fraser

Thomas Y. Crowell Company   New York

Designed by Angela Foote

Manufactured in the United States of America

Library of Congress Cataloging in Publication Data
Batten, Mary.
    The tropical forest.
    SUMMARY: Describes the interrelation of plant and
animal life in a tropical forest.
    1. Forest ecology—Tropics—lit.
[1. Jungle ecology. 2. Ecology] I. Fraser,
Betty, illus. II. Title.
QH541.5.F6B35   574.5'264   73-4196

ISBN 0-690-00138-X
ISBN 0-690-00139-8 (lib. bdg.)

10 9 8 7 6 5 4 3 2 1

To
Alexander
Jenny
Kim
Lori
and
Robert

ACKNOWLEDGMENTS

This book could not have been written without the help of some very dedicated and friendly scientists who are working to understand tropical forests. I am grateful to them for their interest, for taking the time to answer my questions even when my letters pursued them across two continents, and for giving me permission to refer to their work in this book. I am first of all indebted to the Smithsonian Tropical Research Institute (STRI) on Barro Colorado Island, Panama, where most of the research for this book was done and where some of the most original and exciting tropical research in the world is going on. I am especially grateful to Dr. Robert L. Dressler of STRI, who generously gave of his expertise in reading the entire manuscript and making invaluable suggestions for changes and corrections, as did Elmer W. Smith of the Botanical Museum of Harvard University.

For their thoughtful and constructive criticism on specific chapters, thanks to Dr. Martin H. Moynihan, Dr. Michael H. Robinson, Barbara Robinson, Dr. Neal Griffith Smith, and Dr. A. Stanley Rand, all of STRI; Dr. Yoshika Oniki and Dr. Edwin O. Willis of Princeton University; Dr. Philip S. Humphrey, Dr. Martha L. Crump, and Dr. Merlin D. Tuttle of the University of Kansas, Museum of Natural History; Dr. Roger D. Akre of Washington State University; Dr. Charles O. Handley, Jr., of the Smithsonian Institution; Dr. John F. Lawrence of Harvard University; Dr. Peter Marler of the Rockefeller University; and Dr. John R. Oppenheimer of Johns Hopkins University.

Of course the responsibility for the final form of the book is mine alone.

Certain sources were particularly helpful: scientific articles by the scientists mentioned above; the research of Dr. C. H. Dodson and his group at the University of Miami in connection with orchid pollination; and Dr. Paul W. Richards' books, *The Life of the Jungle* and *The Tropical Rain Forest, an Ecological Study*.

Finally, thanks to my editor, Marilyn Kriney, for asking just the right questions and making the kind of demands that helped to give this book its final structure and polish. And thanks to Lothar Wolff for sending me on a marvelous assignment that has resulted, by happy chance, in this book.

Contents

Leaf-cutting ants side by side
with one of the world's largest moths

The Tropical Forest

Life in a Tropical Forest

Tropical forests are not what many of us think they are. They are not the jungles of Tarzan movies and comic books where half-naked people swing through the trees and boil visiting professors for dinner. They are not impenetrable Green Hells filled with terrifying creatures and poison vines waiting to strangle a human victim. The lion, so-called "King of the Jungle," never set foot in a tropical forest except on a Hollywood set.

1

Most of what we think we know about jungles comes from stories by writers who never visited a tropical forest. In such stories imagination runs wilder than any forest creature. These jungles are romantic fictions. They exist mostly in the movies. But real tropical forests are more surprising than any story. Wondrously old and rich with life, they are not like any other forests on earth.

Collected within tropical forests is the greatest variety of plants and animals on earth. From tree roots to treetops the forest teems with life. Three things make this possible: a constant amount of energy from the sun, abundant rainfall, and year-round warmth. These three conditions make tropical forests more favorable to life than any other place on land.

Life began in the ocean, but when living things crawled onto land, they thrived in the warm, moist tropics. Long before the Ice Ages tropical vegetation covered most of the earth's land area. Dinosaurs, which were tropical beasts, roamed freely. Some ate leaves and fruits. Even Antarctica was once covered by tropical trees and plants. A dinosaur's bones found beneath the ice provide evidence of this frigid continent's tropical past.

There is hardly any plant or tree on earth that does not have a tropical ancestor. Even the desert cactus, which thrives in a dry climate completely opposite to that of the humid rain forest, evolved, or developed, from a woody tropical plant. Most land animals, including man, evolved from tropical crea-tures. Anthropologists who study man's family tree trace his ancestry back to apelike animals that lived in the tropical forests of Africa millions of years ago. It is difficult to imagine a time when people did not exist, but clues to such a time are buried in the tropics along with relics of past civilizations.

In some of the world's tropical forests there are ruins of great temples covered with thick vines and twisted roots. The huge stone faces at Angkor Wat in Cambodia are all that remain of the Khmer civilization that flourished more than a thousand years ago. The civilization is dead but the forest survives.

Although they have survived longer than any other collection of vegetation on earth, tropical forests are the last to be studied. In part our ignorance of them has been due to the difficulties of exploring the tropics. Until recently transportation problems, heat, and disease kept all but the most determined naturalists away. In the early years of this century the African rain forest was known as the "white man's grave" because of yellow fever, typhoid, smallpox, and malaria. Today medical science has developed means of controlling these infectious diseases. Yellow fever and typhoid serums and a smallpox vaccination protect the modern traveler. Jet planes connect with riverboats and primitive Indian canoes to reach deep inside the rain forests. Still the great size of a tropical forest, with its endless variety of plants and animals, many of which have not yet been identified, is overwhelming. But scientists all over the world have made a start. Already what they have learned shatters many jungle myths and superstitions. In their place is a growing body of information about the ecology of tropical forests.

Taken from a Greek word, *oikos*, which means "house," ecology is a science that deals with the relationships of living things to each other and to their home. A tropical forest is home to crawling creatures, flying creatures, jumping, slithering, glid-

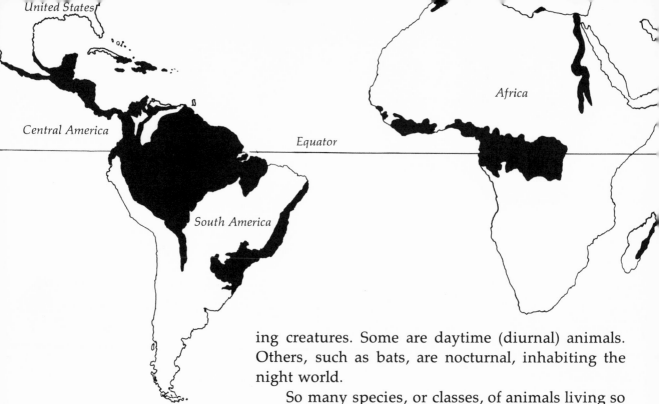

United States

Central America

South America

Equator

Africa

Tropical forests
of the world
(represented by black areas)

ing creatures. Some are daytime (diurnal) animals. Others, such as bats, are nocturnal, inhabiting the night world.

So many species, or classes, of animals living so close together creates great competition for food and space. In meeting this competition animals and plants have developed many different techniques for finding food and defending themselves. Yet life in a tropical forest is not chaotic. It is intricately organized, and the inhabitants of the forest interact in an astonishing variety of ways.

Understanding these interactions is the key to understanding tropical forest ecology. Soil, vegetation, animals, birds, insects—from the smallest bacteria within the soil to the largest prowler among the treetops—all depend on each other in many ways. Survival of the forest depends on these complex interrelationships. They are the heart, pulse, and blood of the forest. A tropical forest is not just a collection of trees but a vast natural system in which living and nonliving things play special parts.

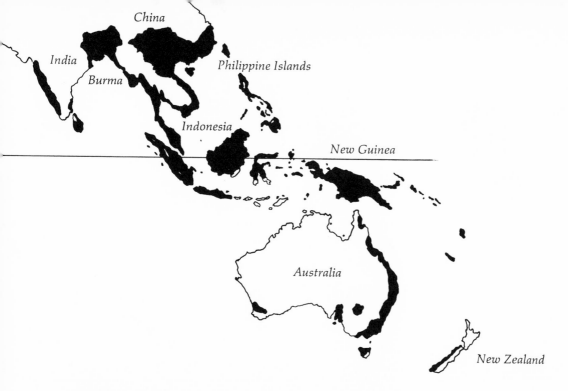

Botanists, biologists who study plants, recognize three main areas of tropical vegetation belting our planet in irregular bands on either side of the equator: the American, the Indo-Malayan, and the African. Together these tropical forests make up half of the earth's wooded area. The American tropics stretch from central Mexico into parts of South America. The Indo-Malayan tropics extend from India and Ceylon through sections of Burma, Thailand, and Indochina, through the Philippines and Indonesia to New Guinea, Australia, and New Zealand. The African tropics are located mostly within the Congo River basin.

These three large geographical areas fall into two divisions: the New World, or American, tropics and the Old World tropics. These divisions are important not only for locating tropical forests but also for identifying their plant and animal life.

Contrary to what many people believe, tropical forests are not all alike. In the Old World tropics there are more land-dwelling, or terrestrial, animals. Old World tropical animals are also larger than those of the New World. Elephants, hippopotamuses, and buffaloes live only in Old World rain forests. In the New World tropics of Central and South America there are more tree-dwelling, or arboreal, animals.

Tropical forests differ according to the amount of rain they receive. Rain forests receive year-round drenchings. The wettest of these is in Cherrapunji, India, where more than four hundred inches of rain fall each year. But a lowland tropical forest in Portuguese Africa receives only fifty or sixty inches of rain a year.

Tropical forests also grow high on mountains where the vegetation is constantly bathed in misty clouds. Cloud forests are found in the mountains of Kenya, New Guinea, Central America, and South America. Here ferns and mosses drip from branches like trains of antique lace.

Cloud forest or rain forest, Old World or New, all tropical forests are strikingly different from the temperate-zone forests that grow between the Tropic of Cancer and the Arctic Circle in the Northern Hemisphere and between the Tropic of Capricorn and the Antarctic Circle in the Southern Hemisphere. Within each hemisphere there is a transition zone that contains both tropical and temperate vegetation. Florida and parts of Louisiana and Texas have a mixed vegetation that botanists call subtropical.

Most of us are familiar with the temperate forests of the Northern Hemisphere, where great stands of one species of tree such as pine, redwood, oak, or maple cover hundreds of acres. In a tropical forest no one species dominates the vegetation. Instead there are thousands of different kinds of trees, but few individuals within each species. In one small area of a tropical forest, acacia, cecropia, balsa, xylosma, gustavia, kapok, jacaranda, symphonia, and many kinds of palms grow side by side with hundreds of other species equally unfamiliar in temperate forests.

In the montane forests of East Africa there are strange, giant plants found no place else on earth. Giant groundsel soars up to thirty feet and giant lobelia to heights of twenty-five feet or more. Even the grass comes in a giant size. Before reaching their full height of thirty or forty feet, mountain bamboo seedlings, members of the grass family, provide food for browsing elephants.

Some areas of tropical Africa contain 25,000 different kinds of plants. But Brazil's Amazon forest has almost twice that number. In one square mile of the Amazon rain forest more than 3,000 species of plants have been found.

The largest tropical forest on earth, the Amazon rain forest, covers an area almost equal to the entire continental United States. Botanists consider the Amazon forest a vast plant museum. But unlike conventional museums, where specimens are stuffed and displayed in glass cases, the Amazon forest is a living collection, continuously growing, changing. Its nearly 3,000,000 square miles contain what some botanists believe to be the oldest forms of vegetation on earth, plants found nowhere else on our planet. Left over from millions of years ago, when glaciers shaved most vegetation off the North Temperate

Giant lobelia

Zone, these plants have the same form as their primitive ancestors.

Because of the Amazon forest's warm, moist climate, old plant forms have been able to survive alongside more recent ones. Plants that could not survive the temperate zone's winter thrive inside tropical forests.

Biologists believe there is a connection between the tropical forest's diversity and its long survival. A temperate forest with only one or two species of trees is often weakened when new organisms are introduced. The most recent serious example of a creature that has upset forest ecology is the gypsy moth. In their home environment, a European forest, gypsy moths cause little damage, for they live in balance with other animals. But in forests in the United States, where they have no predators, gypsy-moth populations have exploded. In the caterpillar stage a gypsy moth eats ten times its weight in leaves each day. Unchecked, these little caterpillars with huge appetites have destroyed thousands of trees and entire forests in the New England states. Scientists and state foresters are still looking for ways to control gypsy moths.

Whenever an organism is taken out of its home community and introduced into a new community, risk is involved. The ecological balance is likely to be upset in the new environment. But a tropical forest is so diverse that it is difficult for a newcomer to upset the balance of life. The greater the variety of plants and animals, the greater the variety of predators, habitats, and food sources. These conditions reduce the likelihood that a newcomer will disturb the ecological balance of an entire forest. The variety of life in a tropical forest seems to give it a built-in immunity. New plants and animals appear and changes in old species occur more easily than in a less diverse forest dominated by one or two species.

Another way that tropical forests are strikingly different from temperate forests is the lack of seasons. Tropical forests have no seasons as we know them —no spring, summer, fall, and winter. All year round the temperature stays near 80 degrees Fahrenheit, with only a few degrees' difference between day and night. In the tropics seasons are measured in inches of rainfall. The months with the heaviest rainfall are called the wet or rainy season. Those with less rain are the dry season. A tropical forest is never as dry as a desert. There is always some moisture, and some forests receive such constant drenchings that there is no dry season at all.

To cope with heavy rains, large leaves have tips like pitcher spouts. A drip tip keeps water from accumulating on the surface, where it could cause the leaf to rot. Drip tips are only one of many details that give a tropical forest a completely different look from a temperate forest.

If you were to fly over a rain forest, you would look down on a thick green mat of vegetation. Here and there tall trees would break through this sea of green, but you would not be able to see the ground as you could if you flew over a temperate forest. Growing closely together, the crowns of rain-forest trees form an almost closed roof that scientists call the "canopy," the uppermost level of the forest. The canopy prevents much light from reaching the ground. Lacking light, the forest floor has little vegetation. It is easy to walk through a rain forest be-

Leaves with drip tips

Buttresses

Stilt roots

cause there is almost no undergrowth, only a thin covering of dead leaves. Thick undergrowth, the kind that men use machetes to hack through, occurs only at the edges of such forests, along river banks, or in clearings made by fallen trees and primitive farmers. Wherever the sun breaks through to the ground, seeds sprout and a rush of green plants stretches toward the light.

In temperate forests branches are low enough to the ground to invite an adventurous climber. In the tropics trees rise like columns for more than fifty feet before branching. The average height of tropical forest trees is one hundred feet, but many soar to two hundred feet or more.

Because the densest growth is farthest from the ground, a tropical forest is top-heavy. Strong winds can topple a tree. As protection against wind, some tropical trees have developed unique means of supporting their heavy tops.

Growing like outspread wings from the bottom of a tree trunk, buttresses, which are really extensions of the trunk, act as props. Found only in the tropics, buttresses help to brace large trees. Other trees, such as mangroves, that live in oozy soil grow stilt roots from the lower part of their trunks. These pitchfork-like prongs give a tree extra support.

Support also comes from lianas, the thick, cable-like vines that grow everywhere in tropical forests. Vines are found in some temperate forests, but the long, trailing variety called lianas grows most abundantly in the tropics. These woody vines begin life on the forest floor, but, like all other forest vegetation, lianas rapidly climb toward the sun as they twist and coil among tree branches. Some lianas are as large around as a man's thigh and many are hundreds of feet long. Woven throughout the canopy, lianas hold the trees like an enormous net spread over the roof of the forest. Held by lianas, trees bend, sway, and sometimes break off from their roots without falling.

In the temperate zone most trees lose their leaves during the fall and winter seasons. These trees are called deciduous, which comes from a Latin word meaning "to fall down." In the tropics most trees are evergreens. They keep their leaves all year round. The life span of a tropical leaf is thirteen or fourteen months. When it falls, another leaf immediately replaces it.

Epiphytes, or air plants, grow everywhere—on tree trunks and branches, even on leaves. Except for mosses, lichens, and ferns, there are no epiphytes in northern temperate forests. In a tropical forest epiphytes are abundant, and they are a striking example of how one group of plants meets the competition for light. Unlike plants that begin their growth on the forest floor, epiphytes begin life in the canopy. Their roots never touch ground. Instead they put out aerial roots, some of which dangle over branches and absorb moisture directly from the humid forest air. With other aerial roots, epiphytes anchor themselves on branches. Most air plants lack a stalk of their own, and use branches for support. Their nutrients come from the small amounts of leaf mold and debris that collect in the crooks of branches and between their own roots. As the leaf mold and debris accumulate, they form real soil. Suspended high above ground, this soil not only feeds epiphytes but also shelters cockroaches,

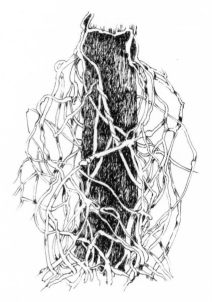

Lianas

Epiphyte

beetles, mites, earthworms, and ants—creatures usually found on the ground.

Unlike animals and plants in the temperate zone, those in the tropics tend to be oversized. Some land turtles weigh more than six hundred pounds. Some moths have a wing span up to twelve inches, and some beetles are as large as a child's fist. Trees are enormous, and the undergrowth is made up of woody plants that look more like trees than the small, bushy herbs of temperate forests. Tropical violets, for example, are the size of apple trees.

Vegetation and climate are the most noticeable differences between a tropical forest and a temperate forest. But there is another difference—the most significant one—and it is invisible. It is hidden in the soil.

In the temperate zone forests can be cleared and the land reforested or planted in crops. Temperate soil is rich in mineral nutrients that new plants need to grow. Most tropical soil is poor. Although at first glance it seems incredible, tropical soil is among the poorest in the world. The reason is the rain. The same water that nourishes life also takes it away. As heavy rains wash over the ground they leach nutrients from the soil, leaving it barren. Yet this impoverished soil supports the most luxuriant vegetation on our planet. A very special kind of cooperation makes this possible.

Over the millions of years that tropical forests have survived, their soil and vegetation have developed a complex way of working together. We cannot see this interaction but we can observe the results. Instead of roots that burrow deep into the ground, tropical trees and plants have shallow roots stretched like outspread fingers just beneath the soil's surface. In a tropical forest this weblike root system is an advantage. Shallow roots can absorb nutrients as soon as they are released into the top-soil without waiting for them to seep down into lower layers of the ground. But shallow roots cannot do all the work by themselves. They have helpers, millions of bacteria and tiny organisms that live on top of and within the soil. These organisms perform one of the most vital functions in the forest—de-composition.

Nutrients which plants need—phosphorus, cal-cium, potassium, and nitrogen—come from the decay of dead animals and vegetation. The decom-posers work continuously, breaking down organisms as soon as they fall to the forest floor. Some decom-posers, or saprovores, as they are called, are too small to be seen with the naked eye. Other decomposers, such as the white and orange fungi similar to north-ern toadstools, are easily visible. Decomposers in tropical forests work so efficiently that almost no dead leaves and animals remain on the ground for more than twenty-four hours.

Decomposers compete with the rains, working to return nutrients to the soil before they are washed away. As fast as decomposition occurs, the shallow roots absorb the minerals, leaving little for the rains.

Unlike a temperate forest, whose minerals are in the soil, a tropical forest's nutrition is locked with-in its vegetation. The nutrients are continually cir-culated and recycled with very little waste. Most of the energy produced by the green plants is returned to them. The energy produced nearly equals the energy that is returned to be reused. Scientists call this a stable system, one that is in balance, or equilibrium.

So long as a tropical forest remains undisturbed, this system works as smoothly and efficiently as the circulatory system in a human body. Tropical forests have perpetuated themselves for millions of years, longer than any other kind of forest. But industrial man has the power to disrupt this special system. Bulldozers cut deep into the forest, severing shallow roots. When a tropical forest is cleared, it cannot be reforested. Nor will its poor soil support farming for more than two or three seasons. Shallow roots are the forest's arteries. When they are cut, the forest dies. No tourniquet can stop its nutrients from flowing down to the river. Stripped of vegetation, a tropical forest is left with only its barren soil.

Power to destroy one of the planet's oldest living systems is industrial man's alone. Indians have lived in tropical forests for untold centuries without destroying them. These small, so-called primitive tribes are as much a part of the forest system as any of its nonhuman inhabitants. Fruit and nut gatherers, such as the Mbuti Pygmies of the African Congo's Ituri Forest, know how to live in harmony with the forest. Their survival has depended on learning the ways of their wooded environment.

To the Pygmies, the forest is sacred. According to the Pygmy creed, "The forest is Mother and Father, because it gives us all the things we need . . . food, clothing, shelter, warmth . . . and affection. We are the children of the forest. When it dies, we die." Outside the Ituri rain forest, the agricultural villagers hate and fear the forest because, like many westerners, they do not understand it.

It would have been more sensible for men to begin their study of forest ecology in the tropical forests where plants originated, but, unfortunately, research began in the temperate forests. As a result it was mistakenly believed that tropical forests could be treated in the same way as temperate forests. Acting out of this erroneous belief, industrial man has destroyed many acres of tropical forest all over the world. Scientists now fear that the great rain forests will be completely destroyed before biologists have a chance to learn what these forests can and do contribute to our world.

Tropical forest scientists are now rushing to make up for lost time, trying to learn all they can before the destruction is complete. Studying a gigantic natural ecological system, or ecosystem, such as a tropical forest is a huge challenge.

Unexpectedly, the Panama Canal helped to advance tropical studies. During the early years of the twentieth century the construction of this canal across the Isthmus of Panama accidentally provided scientists with a custom-made tropical forest laboratory.

In order to build the canal's waterway linking the Atlantic Ocean with the Pacific Ocean, engineers dammed Panama's Chagres River. As the backed-up river water flooded the surrounding valley, many hills were submerged. The higher peaks remained above water level, sticking up like islands in the man-made body of water named Gatun Lake. These new islands were, of course, covered with tropical forest vegetation. From a distance they look like thick bunches of broccoli rising from the lake.

In 1923 the largest of these new islands, Barro

Colorado, was set aside as a scientific reserve. Twenty years later it was acquired by the Smithsonian Institution in Washington, D.C. The Smithsonian, which supports many scientific projects around the world, established a biological research station—the Smithsonian Tropical Research Institute —on Barro Colorado Island. Hunters were forbidden and scientists welcomed. The only shooting allowed was with cameras. Laboratories were built and small cottages constructed. The first director of the Institute reintroduced red spider monkeys to the island, a species that had been hunted to extinction in many areas on Panama's mainland. Today there is a friendly and thriving population of spider monkeys on the island.

With an area of only ten square miles, Barro Colorado is small enough to be explorable. Its boundaries are clear. On one of many well-marked trails, a person can walk from one end of the island to another in a day.

Named for its red soil, Barro Colorado contains the same variety of trees, plants, and animals that

The dotted area represents the Canal Zone. The solid black area is Barro Colorado Island.

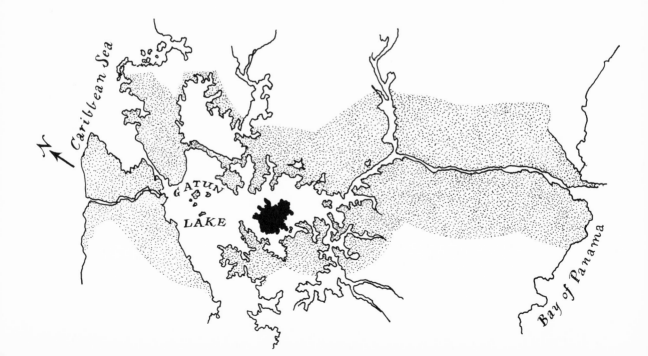

is found in any New World tropical forest. It is a miniature version of a complete tropical forest.

Biologists from all parts of the world come to Barro Colorado to observe a tropical forest at first-hand. Experiments can be set up in this outdoor laboratory. Trees and plants can be identified and classified. Animals are more visible than in a vast mainland forest such as the Amazon.

To a nonscientist, the trees of a tropical forest at first all look alike. Their large, green, leathery leaves seem the same. But you learn to look more closely in the tropics. Your eyes accustom themselves to the dim light beneath the canopy. You begin to notice small details and differences in leaf shape and texture that you never saw before. Your ears also sharpen in this green world that at first seems so silent. Senses alert, you hear the calls of thousands of insects, see the brilliant blue flash of morpho—one kind of butterfly among hundreds—hear the rustle of leaves as monkeys move overhead looking for food, watch a column of small ants moving like an army across the forest floor, and hear the songs of hundreds of species of birds. Inside the forest it is so damp that your clothes stick to your body, but it is strangely cool. You breathe deeply, inhaling sweet, clean air perfumed with the scents of thousands of blossoming plants. Above your head and below your feet there is a myriad of living things.

The forest, like an apartment building, has several stories, each with its own community of plants and animals. But each community depends on green plants. Green plants are basic not only to the ecology of a tropical forest but also to the ecology of our entire planet.

Plants:
Their
Relations
with Animals
and with
Each Other

2

If we could build a machine that worked as efficiently as a green leaf, we would not need to worry about food for our exploding populations. A leaf seems small, fragile, insignificant. In the temperate zone we watch the first tiny leaves appear with spring. During the fall months the leaves turn crimson, yellow, orange, purple before they flutter to the ground in a crusty heap. We don't ordinarily think of leaves as machines, but they are one of the most miraculous ever designed by nature.

Without green leaves, life on earth would be impossible. Only green leaves can transform the sun's energy into food for insects and other animals, including man. Green plants are the producers of our planet. All other organisms are consumers. And every living thing depends on the primary source of energy in our solar system—the sun.

Like a monstrous nuclear reactor, the sun sends out, or radiates, a wide band of energy known as the electromagnetic spectrum. This radiant energy comes to earth in the form of waves of different lengths. Although most of the electromagnetic energy spectrum is invisible, we can detect its presence with sensitive instruments. With infrared photographic film we can take pictures of the energy we feel as heat. With radio telescopes astronomers record radio waves from other planets and distant galaxies. Most of us are familiar with a third part of the electromagnetic spectrum, the invisible ultraviolet rays. We cannot see them but we can see and feel their effects as sunburn. Doctors use X rays to detect broken bones, cavities, and swallowed pennies. Only a tiny portion of the sun's electromagnetic energy is visible to man. This tiny portion, which we call light, illuminates our entire universe. Because our eyes are light-sensitive, we can "see" the world around us. But none of the sun's energy comes to us directly as food.

It would not help us to walk around with our mouths open to the sun. We would only get sunburned tongues. Because we cannot transform light into food by swallowing it or digesting it, we need an intermediary. Green plants alone can do this work.

Three ingredients are necessary to the transformation: water, carbon dioxide, and chlorophyll, the substance that gives a leaf its green color. Water is taken up by a plant's roots. Carbon dioxide comes from the air, and chlorophyll exists within the millions of tiny cells inside a leaf. From water, air, and sunlight, green plants manufacture the energy-rich carbohydrate that we call sugar.

Chemists have just begun to understand how green plants change light energy into chemical energy, or food. This process is called photosynthesis, which comes from two Greek words: *phos*, meaning light; and *synthesis*, meaning to put together. Photosynthesis is so complicated that until recently no one had successfully duplicated it in the laboratory. In the world of the future there may be factories where photosynthesis goes on twenty-four hours a day. Until that time all life on earth will continue to depend on the forests.

But forests cannot operate twenty-four hours a day. Photosynthesis occurs only in the presence of sunlight and at night photosynthesis stops. During the winter months in the temperate zone, when most trees are stripped bare of leaves, photosynthesis takes place only in the relatively few evergreens. In the tropics, however, millions of evergreen plants carry out photosynthesis all year round.

Photosynthesis is the first step in the food web which connects all living things. No matter how varied its diet, every creature on earth depends on green plants.

Many insects and monkeys are vegetarians, feeding directly on green plants. All creatures that

Coreid plant bug,
a first-order consumer

feed on vegetation are first-order consumers. Grazing animals such as sheep and cattle are examples. Their food travels along one pathway—from plant to mouth. Such a food pathway is called a food chain. A vegetarian's food chain is simple, having only one link from plant to animal. But what about the spider that eats insects? What about man who kills cattle for beefsteak and hamburger? We and other creatures who feed on the plant-eaters are second-order consumers. A food chain may have many more links with third-, fourth-, and fifth-order consumers, but all food chains begin with the sun and green plants.

In the process of converting light power into sugar power, green plants contribute something else that is vital to our survival—oxygen. From the broad-leafed evergreens on land to the microscopic phytoplankton in the oceans, wherever green plants carry out photosynthesis, they release oxygen into the atmosphere. The primary producers of the planet also help to create this second essential part of the environment that all living things share.

We and all other animals depend on green plants for food and oxygen. Plants, in turn, depend on animals for the carbon dioxide necessary to carry out photosynthesis. When an animal burns energy, it releases carbon into the atmosphere in the form of carbon dioxide. In the process of breathing we inhale oxygen and exhale carbon dioxide. The exchange of energy between animals and plants is part of the carbon-oxygen cycle. This energy exchange between all living things and their environment is one of life's basic rhythms. It is the battery that powers our biosphere—the sphere on which all life processes, as we know them, occur.

In our biosphere animals and plants are natural allies. One could not do without the other. But the plants came first. Without them, the birds that nest in the branches of trees, the animals that bore into their trunks, the men who eat their fruits and use their wood for construction could not survive.

In a tropical forest the variety of green plants is unforgettable. Because of this diversity there is great competition among plants for the available space and light. Plants also compete in temperate forests, but where there are fewer species competition is not as intense as in a tropical forest.

The strangler fig illustrates how one tropical plant vies with another for a patch of sunlight. The seed of the strangler fig, an epiphyte, sprouts high up in the crevice of a tree. As it grows, the strangler seedling puts out two kinds of roots. One root anchors the plant on its host tree; the other creeps downward, growing closer to the soil. Once it reaches the ground, the long, dangling root acts as a feeding tube drawing nutrients from the soil into the plant. With its supply of nutrients increased, the strangler fig grows rapidly in all directions. In the canopy it puts out more leaves and pushes upward toward the sun. Below, the plant grows more feeding tubes, which gradually encase the host tree on which the strangler has depended for support. As the plant continues to increase in size, its roots thicken, gradually strangling the host tree to death. Completely overgrown with roots, the host tree rots away, leaving a hollow channel within the strangler fig, which has now replaced its host in the canopy.

The struggle between the strangler fig and its host tree is probably the most dramatic example of

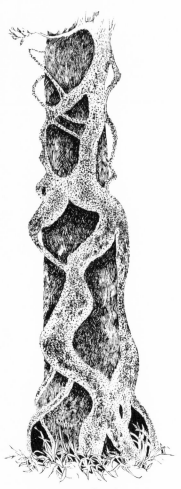

Strangler fig

the relationships between plants as they compete for food and space. But plants also interact with animals, in cooperative as well as competitive ways —and these interactions are necessary for the plant's reproduction.

Because trees and plants cannot move around and mate like animals, many depend on a third party—some creature who can transport the pollen that ensures fertilization and the production of seeds.

Flowers contain a plant's sexual organs: stamens and pistils. The stamen, which can be thought of as the male structure, produces pollen grains. The pistil acts as a female structure. If fertilization is to occur, a whole pollen grain must be transported from the stamen to a pistil of a flower of the same species. Sometimes self-pollination occurs. Sometimes the wind transports pollen, but most flowering plants depend on insects as pollinators.

To attract pollinators, flowering plants evolved brightly colored and sweet-smelling blossoms. Inside a tropical forest you can always find a flower in bloom all year round. There are red, yellow, orange, fuchsia, purple, even speckled blossoms, each with its own particular perfume to attract a pollinator. But plants need more than color and scent to lure a pollinator deep within the blossom where the pollen grains lie. Nectar, a sweet secretion inside a blossom, serves this purpose. A sweet-tasting food for many forest creatures—bees, bats, even monkeys—nectar serves the purpose of the plant while providing food for insects and other animals.

While going after nectar, an animal brushes against the stamen. Pollen grains stick to its body. Moving to another blossom for another drink of nectar, the animal becomes a living powder puff, dusting pistils with pollen grains.

Trees and plants that depend on pollinators have developed a variety of flowering patterns designed to attract the creatures so crucial to their reproduction. Some trees compete for the attention of pollinators by producing flowers directly from their bark, where the insects can find them easily. In a tropical forest it is not unusual to see blossoms on a bare tree trunk. This type of flowering, which occurs mostly in the tropics, is called cauliflory. Many other tropical trees depend on nectar-eating bats for pollination. These trees have evolved pendulous blossoms, which are easier for bats to locate as they navigate through the forest at night.

Some of the most complicated and unusual blossoms are found among orchids. The largest family of flowering plants, orchids make up nearly a seventh of all such plants on earth. For centuries orchids have been highly prized, subjects of superstition and mystery. The ancient Greeks mistakenly believed that orchids were a powerful aphrodisiac, capable of arousing passionate desire. This old superstition carries over in the modern custom of giving an orchid to a very special person, a custom that has made orchid cultivation a multimillion-dollar business. But there are also people who prize orchids for their beauty. Societies of these orchid fanciers exist throughout the world.

Although 25,000 species of these strange and beautiful plants are already known, new species continue to be discovered. Some bloom for less than a day. Orchids come in all the colors of the rainbow, but some colors are found among very few plants.

Cauliflory,
on the trunk of
a cacao tree

These rare orchids—rare because of their color—sell for hundreds of dollars.

Although most orchids grow in the tropics, they are found on every continent except Antarctica. Some are found high in the mountains, some in water, and at least two grow underground. Some tropical orchids grow on the ground and others belong to the group of plants known as epiphytes (air-plants) that anchor themselves on branches often more than sixty feet above ground. The variety of orchid shapes, sizes, and colors is fantastic and even bizarre. You may think you are looking at a moth, a bee, or a butterfly when you are really staring at an orchid. The design of each blossom has evolved along with a certain type of pollinator. In many cases orchid flowers seem custom-made to fit the body of a hummingbird, a moth, or a bee. One orchid even resembles a female wasp. A male wasp, attempting to mate with the flower, picks up pollen masses which he transports to the next blossom.

In Central and South America 2,000 species of orchids depend on a family of jewel-colored bees for pollination. Iridescent green, blue, and gold, the Euglossine bees, a family related to honey bees and bumble bees, are attracted by a variety of perfumes produced by the orchids. Only the male Euglossine bees follow these scents, and only certain scents attract particular bees. Several dozen different fragrances have been identified. Some smell like women's perfumes. One smells like Vicks VapoRub, and another like oil of wintergreen.

At the Smithsonian Tropical Research Institute, Dr. Robert Dressler, a biologist who studies orchids, discovered that different species of bees are attracted

Euglossine bee
and one of the orchids
it pollinates

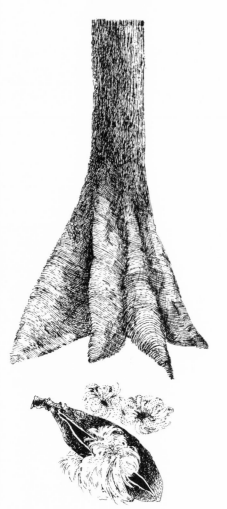

Trunk and seed of kapok tree

to different scents. In an experiment he dipped small squares of blotting paper in various scents and then attached the squares to tree trunks. Within an hour Euglossine bees had swarmed onto the squares. Just as with the real orchids, each scented paper square attracted only certain bees.

Why orchid perfumes attract bees is a mystery —one of the many mysteries of tropical forests that remain to be solved by scientists. These orchids do not provide food for the bees, yet they collect the perfumes and store them in their hollow hind legs. Biologists like Dr. Dressler hope to discover just how bees use the perfume. Whatever the answer, the attraction of bees to an orchid's scent plays a vital part in the plant's reproduction. As a bee gathers perfume, compact masses of pollen grains stick to its body. When the bee flies to another orchid blossom to gather more perfume, the pollen is transported to the flower's stigma and fertilization takes place. Such interactions between animals and vegetation are necessary for the forest's survival.

In addition to attracting pollinators, vegetation also takes advantage of the weather. In a seasonal tropical forest such as that of Barro Colorado, many trees drop their fruits at the end of the dry season. When the rains come, the seeds are already on the ground, ready to use the increased moisture for sprouting. Some seeds are even encased in a gauzy envelope that holds moisture until the heavy rains come.

Certain trees make use of the dry season to produce wing-shaped or fluff-topped seeds which are easily carried by the wind to the ground. The kapok tree's seeds, for example, are topped by soft wads of fluff which are easily borne by the wind. This same fluff is used to stuff cushions and life preservers. The kapok produces an abundance of seeds for reproduction, and the seeds also serve as food for parakeets. These tiny, colorful birds make a steady chorus of sound as they perch among the kapok's branches. Because parakeets eat so many of the kapok's seeds, the tree must overproduce to keep from being eaten out of existence.

Interactions between animals and vegetation occur in all forests, but in a tropical forest these relationships are more varied, more complex, and more subtle because of the immense variety of competition. At the same time, competition creates pressure for animals and plants to improve themselves.

If an athlete has ten competitors, he must develop more skills than he would need if he had only one. The same is true of animals, insects, birds, and plants in a tropical forest. More competition creates more pressure for developing more skills to meet the competition. Biologists call this "evolutionary pressure." Plants and animals that meet such pressure successfully have usually evolved ingenious ways of adapting, or adjusting, to a variety of different conditions. Tropical forest plants and animals are flexible, changeable, capable of surviving in many ways rather than in only one way.

Taken as a whole system, the tropical forest is like a team of athletes trained to meet all possible competition. The variety of forest life, animal and vegetable, is its most demanding coach. The vegetation is its clubhouse, training ground, and playing field, but the game is serious—a competition for survival itself.

Layers
of
Life

3

In a tropical forest so many creatures live so closely together that every inch of space is a home, a habitat, for something. Baby caterpillars cluster on the undersides of leaves. Spiders spin their webs between trees and vines. Rainwater in broken fruit shells houses mosquito larvae. Grubs bore into palm fruits, and ants seem to crawl on every available exposed surface.

Even an animal's back can be home to other

creatures. Sloths, for example, have long, shaggy hair, and each hair has grooves to which tiny algae, vegetable hitchhikers, cling. Algae, in turn, are tasty food for moth larvae that also live on the sloth's back. Neither the algae nor the moth larvae are parasites. They are not completely dependent on the sloth for both food and shelter. Algae and moth larvae simply use sloths as mobile homes. Algae even help the sloth by giving its fur a greenish tint that blends in with the leaves and camouflages the animal as it eats, sleeps, mates, and even gives birth hanging upside down from a tree branch.

Sloth

Through this and similar living arrangements animals make use of every crack and corner in the forest. From its roots to its leafy roof, a tropical forest teems with life.

Like an apartment building, a tropical forest has many stories. Scientists divide a tropical forest into four main levels—ground level, low forest, mid-forest, and canopy.

The ground level includes the surface and subsurface of the soil. Below the soil leaf-cutting ants grow fungus gardens and hairy tarantulas burrow. The forest floor seems bare but it provides habitats for many creatures. In addition to the fungi, bacteria, mites, and insects that decompose dead leaves and animals, there are a multitude of other ground-floor dwellers. In a New World tropical forest many species of large rodents—guinea pig–like creatures such as pacas and agoutis—live on the forest floor. There are also small armadillos; peccaries, the only wild pigs in the hemisphere; and coatimundis, relatives of the North American raccoon.

The ground floor is also a nursery for plant and

tree seedlings. Although most seedlings are green, the first tiny leaves of a number of tropical plants and trees are brilliant red or crimson because they contain so little chlorophyll. As the plants grow upward, competing for light, their leaves broaden and become leathery. The stalks of trees become slender trunks.

A few feet above the ground, shrubs make up the low forest level where many insects and even some birds live. Unlike the small shrubs that grow in temperate forests, tropical shrubs resemble dwarf

Canopy

Mid-forest level

Low forest level

Ground level

trees. In between the low forest and the canopy is the mid-forest level, where tall, straight tree trunks soar skyward. Splotched with mosses and lichens, the trunks are fine places for beetles, caterpillars, and moths to hide during the day. So perfectly do these creatures blend with the bark, they are almost invisible. What seems to be a patch of rough bark may turn out to be a colony of bees that can lift off like a squadron of phantom jets and sting an intruder. The space between the ground and the canopy is largely open, providing flying room for birds.

The topmost level of the forest, the canopy, it-self contains low, middle, and upper layers of vege-tation. Trees that can grow in shadier places stand below the upper canopy. These shade-tolerant spe-cies top off at fifty or sixty feet, forming the lowest layer of the canopy. Often this understory is so thick that from the ground you cannot see the upper can-opy. Other trees top off at a hundred feet, forming the middle layer of the canopy. A third group, with spreading umbrella-like crowns, soars up to two hundred feet, breaking through the dense, almost closed canopy like periscopes rising above the sur-face of the sea.

If you stand on the deck of a boat and look at a tropical forest from a distance, you can see the differ-ent canopy layers formed by trees of various heights. Together, the layers of the lower, middle, and upper canopy act like the roof of a greenhouse, trapping and holding heat and moisture inside the forest. For this reason the temperature of the forest interior hardly changes from night to day.

The canopy is a special world. Because it re-ceives the most light, the canopy is the most favor-able level of the forest for plants. Nestled among branches and lianas high above ground are an amaz-ing variety of orchids, ferns, peppers, and brome-liads, prickly-leaved plants that are members of the pineapple family. Bromeliads are the most con-spicuous epiphytes in a tropical forest but they are difficult to collect because they grow so far above ground. Some botanists have battle scars from peri-lous climbs to reach a bromeliad. Others collect from a safer distance, using a gun to shoot down branches laden with the prickly plants. The most ingenious method is to train a monkey to do the collecting. Botanists are interested in bromeliads because they are mini-ecosystems, important to dozens of tiny creatures. When it rains, bromeliads fill up with water like tanks. Sometimes bromeliad tanks collect as much as four and a half quarts of water, creating treetop ponds where water beetles, snails, and frogs live and breed.

On Barro Colorado, as in other New World tropical forests, more than half the animals live in the canopy. Monkeys and many species of birds share the treetops with tree frogs, tree snakes, lizards, sloths, adult iguanas, and various colonies of insects.

Canopy life is difficult to observe because it is so far from the ground. But in the Guama Ecological Reserve in Belém, Brazil, a tower was constructed to give scientists and wildlife photographers a direct view into this leafy habitat.

Morning in the canopy is filled with the sounds of animals waking, communicating with each other, and stirring through branches as they begin to search for food. Some canopy animals and birds range freely from one layer to another. Others spend most of their time in only one layer.

Howler monkeys stay in the upper canopy and come to the ground only to rescue a fallen infant. Cebus monkeys range throughout the canopy along with spider monkeys, who swing from layer to layer and sometimes even come to the ground.

In the canopy of the Old World rain forest in Africa there are many flying and gliding creatures found no place else—scaly-tailed flying squirrels, a creature called a tree pangolin that eats termites and ants, and several species of lemurs, which

Tree pangolin

are the most primitive monkeys on earth. But the most spectacular leaper of the African rain forest is the colobus monkey. This long-haired, black and white animal seems almost to fly through the trees.

In both Old and New World tropical forests the birds of the upper canopy treat the treetops as their ground level and rarely penetrate into the forest below.

Part forest, part sky, the top of the canopy contrasts sharply with the still, dark world below. Breezes continually rustle the leaves and stir the air. Unsheltered, the top of the forest absorbs not only the most light but also the heaviest amount of moisture. Some rainwater never reaches the ground but is held by leaves, epiphytes, and crevices in the enormous branches—sometimes six feet around—of upper canopy trees.

In contrast to the size of their limbs, trees in the upper canopy tend to have smaller, in some cases more feathery leaves than trees in the lower canopy. On top of the forest, where the sun is brightest, light absorption takes place easily. Below, in the dim forest interior, trees and plants need the largest light-absorbing surfaces possible. Their leaves are usually broad and leathery.

At each level of a tropical forest, from its canopy to its floor, the vegetation creates millions of habitats, places where animals can make their homes. By interacting with the vegetation, creatures in all the forest's habitats play different roles in the forest's ecology. The relationships that an animal has with its habitat make up what scientists call its "ecological niche."

Niche means more than just a place. It refers

both to place and to what an animal does within and to its place. Just as a habitat is an animal's address in the forest, a niche is an animal's job. In any ecosystem, whether a forest or a city, there are certain basic niches, or jobs, that must be filled: food production, food consumption, decomposition, and population control. In a tropical forest some animals act as decomposers, some as pollinators, all as consumers participating in numerous food chains. Plants fill the role of producers, as we have seen.

Human ecosystems, such as a city, have the same niches. Food must be produced, wastes removed, and births controlled so that a population explosion will not occur.

In cities people are the dominant species. People occupy all the ecological niches. Other animals, such as pet dogs and cats, are forced to live in human habitats—houses and apartments. The unwanted animals—mice, rats, cockroaches—live out their lives foraging among garbage cans and sidewalk litter. Some cities are so overcrowded with people that there are no niches for newcomers.

In a tropical forest no one species dominates all the others. Intense competition for survival prevents population explosions. Because there is such a great variety of species, habitats, and niches, a new arrival doesn't endanger the forest. It simply finds a new niche.

Some people think of cities as concrete jungles, but there are more differences between cities and tropical forests than there are similarities. Far from being balanced ecosystems like a tropical forest, our cities are increasingly unbalanced, threatened by population explosions, waste, pollution, and crime.

If tropical forests were as chaotic as our sprawling megalopolises, survival would be difficult, perhaps impossible. But forest life has evolved in very organized ways. The arrangement of life in vertical layers—from ground to treetops—is one kind of organization that contributes to the working of the whole forest system. But this organization, like many other things in a tropical forest, is not obvious to the onlooker. Staying alive in the forest often depends on being able to hide and stay hidden. The leaves are covers for thousands of eyes.

Techniques
for
Survival

When foraging or gather-
ing food, animals participate in one of the principal
ecological relationships in any ecosystem: the relationship between predators—hunters that kill for
food—and their prey, or victims. Unlike vegetarians,
who feed directly on vegetables, fruits, grains, and
nuts, predators are carnivores. They feed on flesh.
In the web of life predators are consumers of the
second, third, fourth, fifth, or sixth order, or even
higher.

4

The organization of life between predators and prey is not a simple division between the good guys and the bad guys. For any animal, food is one of life's necessities. People obtain food by farming, ranching, and fishing. Some people are strict vegetarians, first-order consumers. The rest of us are carnivores. Like other predators, we also kill for food.

People eat almost anything. Cattle, sheep, horses, chickens, pigs, whales, fish, snails, rattlesnakes, bullfrogs, ants, and grasshoppers are part of some human being's diet somewhere on this planet. Among tribes of cannibals, men have even eaten their own kind. Death is an inescapable part of predator-prey relationships. Even man was once hunted for food. Fifteen thousand years ago our Stone Age ancestors were preyed upon by wolf packs, crocodiles, and some of the large cats. Tools and intelligence freed people from their role as prey for these animals. Today man is the most powerful predator on earth. Many extinct and endangered animals, such as the pygmy chimpanzee and the imperial parrot, are sad evidence of man's power to erase an entire species from the surface of the earth. Of course, people have protected some animals. Few Americans would think of eating "man's best friend." Horsemeat hamburgers and steaks are still eaten in parts of Europe, but in the United States man has always had a special relationship with his horse. In western movies, the "horse operas," cowboys shared star billing with their steeds. In India cows are sacred animals, leading privileged lives in cities where hundreds of thousands of Indians starve. Religion, sentiment, and cultural taboos are only a few of many reasons that lead men to protect certain animals. There are also various reasons for hunting and killing animals. Food is, of course, the main reason, but people also kill animals for their fur or simply for sport. Only in an ecosystem undisturbed by man is the relationship between hunters and their victims solely a result of the competition for food.

In a simple ecosystem with only a few species, the roles of predator and prey are clear. In a barn where there are cats and mice, there is one predatory group and one prey group. In this case cats are the predators. They benefit immediately from the predator-prey relationship. But what about the future of such a simple system?

In time both cat and mouse populations would increase through the natural process of reproduction. But the mouse population would always have to stay ahead of the cats. Unless the mice reproduced enough young both to ensure their own survival as a species and to satisfy their predators' appetites, the cats would soon eat all the available mice. If this happened, the cats would have no food supply and eventually they would die.

A similar situation exists in countries where the human population has outgrown food production. When there is not enough food to go around, people suffer from hunger and die of malnutrition and starvation.

Balance is the key to a smoothly running ecosystem, whether that system be a barnyard, a tropical forest, a city, or an entire planet. Predator and prey populations must achieve a balanced relationship if an ecosystem is to survive.

In a complex system such as a tropical forest,

many animals have double roles in the prey-predator relationship. Because of the intense competition for food, they are both hunter and hunted. As with people, there are few examples of cannibalism. Mostly, animals hunt species other than their own, and usually they kill only for food and to protect their young. Some weasels, however, are known to go on killing frenzies in which they kill many more prey than they can eat.

Size plays a part in predator-prey relationships. Few animals willingly tangle with others bigger than themselves. Within their own natural environments, elephants, lions, jaguars, and whales have no predators. Yet some of these creatures are endangered species, threatened by an invading predator whose weapons make up for what he lacks in size. Already several species of whales are extinct, victims of overkill by the whaling industry. Of course, as a result, the whaling industry is also virtually extinct. But before it disappears completely, the industry is going after one final victim, the blue whale. This magnificent beast, the largest animal that ever lived on this planet, is now endangered by a creature it dwarfs—man.

Fur hunters have seriously threatened South American jaguars, and leopards of Old World tropical forests. Hunting and the destruction of their habitats endanger Africa's pygmy hippopotamus and Central America's tapir. Inside Barro Colorado's tropical forest, spider monkeys have no predators. But in many areas of Panama's mainland, men have hunted spider monkeys to extinction.

There is nothing to check man's predation except his own intelligence and his concern for the world

Tapir

Pygmy hippopotamus

he inhabits. In a tropical forest there are natural checks and balances. Predator-prey populations are controlled by disease, parasites, and death from old age, but the most effective agent of population control is the availability of food. When food is abundant, a species usually increases in number. When food is scarce, fewer members of a species can survive. In many cases a rise and fall in predator population is directly related to a rise and fall in prey population.

Small creatures such as insects, which are a source of food for many animals including other insects, have the greatest number of predators. Yet insects outnumber all other classes of animals on our planet. Inside a tropical forest insects are found at every level—on the ground, in shrubs, beneath leaves, among branches, inside fruits, and on the backs of other animals. Night and day you can hear the buzzes and hums of thousands of insects. Because they reproduce at an enormous rate and because they have an amazing variety of ingenious defenses, insects have survived for millions and millions of years.

In a tropical forest survival depends on finding food, whether plant or animal, and, at the same time, on escaping from predators. Because neither predator nor prey wins all the time, no tropical forest species is threatened by extinction or by a population explosion. Unlike our own species, whose population threatens to overrun the earth, no one group of predators in a tropical forest endangers the survival of an entire species.

Because a tropical forest contains such a variety of creatures, it is very difficult to upset the balance between predator and prey populations. But just as the less diverse ecosystems of North American temperate forests have been upset by the gypsy moth, so predator-prey relationships in tropical areas outside the forest have also been unbalanced when a new species has been introduced.

In 1872 four pairs of mongooses—long, slender, catlike animals—were brought from India to Hawaii and the West Indies. The animals were introduced on these islands in the hope that they would destroy the rats that were eating sugar cane. The mongooses did their job too well. Within ten years they were pests. After reducing the rat population to a low level, it was easy for the mongooses, whose population had been increasing, to turn to toads, lizards, birds, and mammals. Because they were newcomers to the island ecosystems, the mongooses had no predators to control their population. The introduction of mongooses upset the already existing ecological relationships between predators and prey.

In a tropical forest each predator endangers some lives but does not upset the balance of life.

During the millions of years that tropical forest species evolved in their special environment, they developed their own tricks for survival. Although many variations exist, there are three principal ways of getting along with one's enemies: camouflage, cooperation, and threats.

People also use each of these three methods, not always for survival. Anyone who has dressed up on Halloween night is familiar with camouflage. Masks and costumes are dandy disguises for playing trick or treat. Criminals, spies, and movie stars may have a wardrobe of disguises. Wigs, phony beards and

Mongoose

mustaches, dark glasses, and even plastic surgery are used to make a person unrecognizable. During wartime, camouflage is a matter of life and death. To conceal themselves from their enemies, soldiers wear specially colored clothes, cover their artillery with leaves and branches, and in general try to blend into the background.

The second method of survival, cooperation, is used at every level of human life, in the family and in international relations. People and nations form cooperative alliances and make treaties to protect themselves against those they consider their enemies.

When cooperation doesn't work or seems impossible, people use a third method of survival: threats. This method is riskier than the other two because a threat may not scare off an enemy. If it doesn't, violence can erupt. In spite of the risk, great nations like the United States and the Soviet Union still threaten each other with their stockpiles of deadly weapons. Less serious threat-making goes on among children at play. Screaming, making faces, jumping up and down, shaking fists, and throwing things are all forms of threats used by human children and animals of other species, particularly monkeys.

In the world of a tropical forest camouflage, cooperation, and threat are part of the natural rhythms of life.

Camouflage is a vivid example of evolution at work. Over the long periods of time that species have lived in tropical forests, some animals have taken on the colors and shapes of the vegetation they live among. To the naked eye, the animal looks exactly like a part of its habitat. A leopard, for ex-

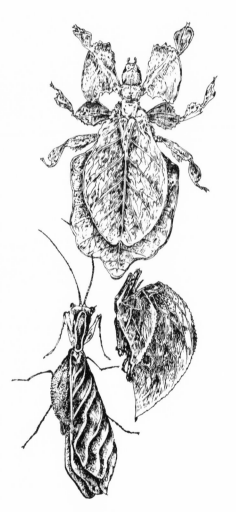

Leaf mimics

ample, is almost invisible crouched in the canopy because its spots look like the dappled patterns of leaf shadows. Moths also benefit from spots. To startle predators, moths spread their wings, revealing spots that can be mistaken for the eyes of a larger animal.

Leaf mimics, a large group of tropical forest insects including such species as katydids and mantids, are a striking example of camouflage. Lying motionless against twigs and small branches, these little creatures blend in perfectly with the leaves. Unless they move, leaf mimics are invisible to all except the trained eye of a scientist or the sharp eye of a predator. Marked with tiny leaflike veins and dew spots, the bodies of leaf mimics are almost exact copies of leaves. Just as there are many different shapes of leaves in a tropical forest, so there are a great variety of leaf mimics.

Their imitation of leaves does not stop with color and shape. When walking, a leaf mimic sways from side to side, imitating the motion of a leaf stirred by a gentle breeze. Entomologists—biologists who study insects—refer to the way a leaf mimic moves as "cryptic walking." "Cryptic" comes from a Greek word meaning "hidden." Entomologists use this word to describe a leaf mimic's movement because cryptic walking is part of the insect's disguise, helping to hide it from its predators.

During the day leaf mimics are still. At night, when it is dark and they cannot be seen as easily, they move around looking for food.

Not all leaf mimics are green. One variety is the color of a dry, dead, brown leaf. Suspended on the underside of a twig, the dead-leaf mimic, as it is called, would fool anyone. Although small, this mimic can threaten a larger predator. By unfolding its colored wings, the dead-leaf mimic suddenly looks bigger, almost twice its normal size. If the threat is successful, the startled predator moves to another hunting ground. If the threat doesn't work, there is one really dead leaf mimic.

A few creatures that aren't insects also look like leaves. Among them are leaf-mimicking toads and fish that mimic dead leaves drifting in the water.

Leaf mimicry is an example of forest camouflage. Another is found among a group of insects called walking sticks. If you were to look closely at a bush or the end of a branch, you might stare a walking stick straight in the eye without knowing it. Some walking sticks are green like some forest twigs. Other walking sticks are the color of brownish gray twigs. Like leaf mimics, walking sticks are nocturnal (nighttime) creatures. During the day they lie motionless, invisible among the foliage of forest shrubs.

Entomologists who collect walking sticks for study go into the forest at night. Collecting at night is quite an adventure. As soon as the sun sets the forest becomes black. The sounds of the day are replaced by the sounds of night creatures foraging. You are surrounded by thousands and thousands of animals that you cannot see.

Essential for night collecting is a head light, but not the kind found on a car. You wear this light on your head like a miner. Before going into the forest, you check your batteries to make sure your head light works. You take a few extra batteries in your pocket. In Panama you rub your arms and face with mosquito repellent before starting down one of the

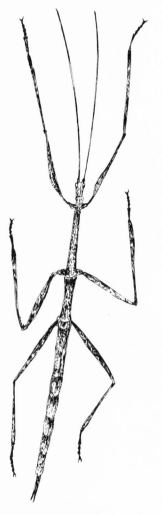

Walking stick

forest trails. Your head light cuts a narrow strip through the blackness, and you walk cautiously along your avenue of light. You carefully inspect shrubs as you search for camouflaged insects.

To see a walking stick move is to watch a motionless thing come alive. Tiny stick-like legs unfold from a long stick body. The legs begin to move as the creature crawls toward a leaf, on which it will feed.

British zoologist Dr. Michael Robinson and his wife, Barbara, who made a study of walking sticks and leaf mimics on Barro Colorado Island, observed that these insects defend themselves in several ways. Through camouflage, they hide among twigs and leaves or play dead. But some species also use startle mechanisms; they make themselves look larger and more threatening by suddenly flashing colored wings and rising up on their back legs. These colored wings are usually folded flat against a walking stick's body. If disturbed, the insect unfolds its wings and rubs them together. The rubbing, which is called "stridulation," produces a rough, grating noise. Sometimes the noise and sight of the wings will scare off a predator.

Still another defense used by stick insects and leaf mimics is a vile-tasting or vile-smelling secretion. Like a skunk, some insects spray their pursuers with a noxious perfume. The scent is a kind of reverse advertisement, warning a predator that a bad-smelling creature couldn't possibly taste all that good.

Skunks are also an example of another kind of defense that is just the opposite of camouflage—warning coloration. Using this survival technique, an animal protects itself by being constantly conspicuous. At first this seems strange. How can an animal defend itself and attract a predator's attention at the same time?

If an animal is particularly poisonous, it sometimes advertises the fact in order to warn predators to keep their distance. The skunk's bold black and white pattern is a warning to stay away from its smelly spray. Similarly, many tropical animals advertise their nastiness by wearing bright colors.

The most brilliantly colored tropical butterflies are usually the most bitter-tasting—no fit meal for a hungry bird. Poison-arrow frogs, whose paralyzing venom is used by South American Indians to make poison-tipped arrows, look like forest jewels with their red, orange, purple, green, and black patterns. But even touching the frogs' skin can cause severe pain, because the poison is secreted by glands in the skin. The bright red, yellow, and black candy-striped pattern of the coral snake warns predators to avoid this venomous creature of the forest floor.

The bolder the colors and patterns, the more easily a predator learns to leave the poisonous creature alone.

Taking advantage of warning coloration, many harmless species have evolved colors and patterns that mimic the nastier species. Several kinds of butterflies mimic the bitter-tasting varieties. And almost eighty species of harmless snakes mimic coral snakes.

Animals thus use mimicry for two purposes: to be noticed and to hide. Both are important survival devices.

What works for the hunted also works for the hunters. Predators use camouflage to trick their intended victims. Draped among branches, several species of snakes resemble vines. When a vine snake

Poison-arrow frog

comes within striking distance of its prey, it slithers along its perch and quickly captures an unwary victim such as a tree frog.

Although most camouflage is visual, there is at least one kind in a tropical forest that is vocal. This may seem surprising, since the slightest sound can give away an animal's hiding place to some sharp-eared predator. Animals are usually quiet, particularly during daylight. But one species of forest falcon uses its call as part of its hunting technique. Like a ventriloquist, the falcon throws its voice, disguising its location. This forces birds it preys on to seek it out so as to avoid being taken by surprise. But it's a risky operation. Prey birds must change position in such a way as to spot the falcon without the falcon's spotting them. A Barro Colorado scientist, Dr. Neal Griffith Smith, has discovered that the prey birds disguise their locations by using a technique that is similar to that of the falcon but not exactly the same. Instead of throwing their voices like the falcon, prey birds call in a way that makes it difficult for the falcon to pinpoint their locations. Neither the falcon nor its prey successfully disguises its location all the time. When a prey bird shows itself, that's usually the end of the line. The falcon takes advantage of the opportunity to capture its next meal.

Camouflage is one of nature's marvelous designs. From the arctic polar bear, whose dazzling white fur blends in with its habitat of snow and ice, to the tropical leaf mimic, animals large and small have developed ways of hiding. In any forest anywhere on earth there are examples of camouflage, but a greater variety can be found in a tropical forest because of its diversity of living things.

Camouflage is sometimes used with a second method of survival, cooperation. Finding greater safety in numbers, swallowtail caterpillars clump together on tree trunks and mimic patches of bark. If a predator touches them, swallowtail caterpillars use two other defenses. First they stick out pairs of yellowish horns, transforming themselves into a clump of tiny monsters. Next they produce a vile odor that temporarily fills an area around the tree. The more caterpillars, the stronger the scent and the greater the possibility of scaring off predators.

Group cooperation is found among monkeys, birds, bees, ants, and other species that live in societies. Being a member of a group gives an animal greater protection against predators and, at the same time, advantages in hunting prey. Like camouflage, cooperation serves a double purpose, helping an animal in its double role as predator and prey.

Cooperation also exists between animals and vegetation. In the top layer of the canopy, some ants and orchids share a relationship that benefits each. The seeds of an orchid sprout and grow in an ants' nest. As the plant increases in size it forms a mass of roots, which the ants use to enlarge their nest. In turn, the orchid receives some nutrition from the nest. There is also another benefit. Orchids are vulnerable to everything that eats plants—crickets, grubs, and slugs. Ants prey on these creatures and protect the orchids from predation.

The third method of survival, making threats, involves what scientists call "threat postures" or "threat displays." When making threats, an animal usually arranges its body or mouth into certain positions.

Howler monkey

Monkeys use a great variety of threatening facial expressions, sounds, and body movements. Male howler monkeys threaten with a powerful roar that can be heard miles away. Like the dog whose bark is more ferocious than his bite, the male howler keeps would-be intruders at a distance with his roar. But it is quite rare to see howler monkeys actually fighting. A smaller monkey, the cebus, threatens by jumping up and down and opening its mouth in a wide, toothy grimace. Female iguanas, members of the reptile family, threaten by opening their mouths wide and forcefully exhaling to produce a loud sound.

If a threat doesn't frighten a predator, a prey animal must be prepared to defend itself. Some defenses are built into the body designs of creatures. A hairy caterpillar seems to be nothing more than a patch of moving white fluff, but its tiny, furry hairs cause itching and stinging if touched. With a popping sound and a puff of "smoke," the bombardier beetle defends itself with a sudden spray from its abdomen—a chemical spray that can leave a predator nursing painful burns.

One of the most unusual of such defenses is that of a crab that lives near tropical forest streams.

This species, which is found on Barro Colorado, looks exactly like those we find along the edges of beaches in the Northern Hemisphere, but there is a great difference. Most crabs live and breathe in water, but this tropical species is a land creature with a unique defense—a self-amputating leg. When attacked, this land crab will pinch and hold its attacker with the claw at the end of one of its legs. Then the crab releases its leg and scuttles away to safety, leaving the surprised predator painfully trapped by a naked claw. Sometime later the crab grows another leg.

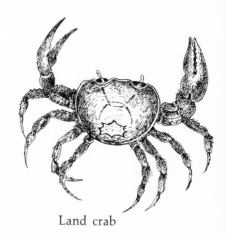

Land crab

Tropical forest animals may do anything to defend themselves and to capture food. There are no limits on survival methods. Trickery and surprise are important in the continuous game of hide-and-seek that goes on between predators and prey, and the females of one species of tropical spiders use both. During the daytime the female spider mimics a stick. At night she moves, getting into position to trap ants as they pass underneath her web. Then she spins a tiny net which she holds stretched between her two front legs. As an ant crawls within range, the spider, with surprising speed, dabs the sticky net against her prey. This unusual hunting technique gives the spider its name—the web-throwing spider.

Depending on how it captures food, a predator can increase its survival advantage over other species who compete for the same food. Dr. Michael Robinson, who has spent many years studying the complex relationships among tropical forest animals, discovered a species of silver-backed spiders on Barro Colorado Island that has a distinct survival advantage. The females of this species use one method to capture moths and butterflies and another to capture grasshoppers and crickets. If a grasshopper or cricket falls into a silver-backed spider's web, the female immediately wraps the insect in thin silk strands that she spins from her body. After wrapping her prey, the spider bites it. She leaves her packaged food in the web until she is hungry. But if a moth or a butterfly falls into her web, first she bites, then she wraps the insect.

Observing that the spider used these two different methods, Dr. Robinson wondered why the spider bit moths before wrapping and wrapped grasshoppers before biting. Obviously the spider could tell the difference between the two kinds of prey, but not, as one might think, by eyesight, for most spiders have poor vision. Whatever means the spider was using to identify its prey, Dr. Robinson knew she had a survival advantage over other species of spiders that do not discriminate. The reason is that butterflies and moths have scales on their wings which help them to escape from spider webs. By biting first, the silver-backed spider immediately stuns these prey, preventing their escape.

Dr. Robinson experimented to learn how the silver-backed spider could tell which of the insects had fallen into her web. There were several possibilities: web vibration, odor, and touch. First he tested web vibration. When butterflies or moths fall into a web, their wings make the web vibrate differently than it does if a grasshopper falls into it. Putting a grasshopper on the tip of a long needle attached to a vibrator, Dr. Robinson introduced it into a web. The vibrator made the web shake as it does when a moth or butterfly falls into it. As usual the spider rushed from the center of her web to the vibrating grasshopper. As usual she wrapped, then bit the insect. Clearly web vibration was not the spider's clue to its prey's identity.

Next Dr. Robinson tested for touch. For this part of the experiment he disguised the moth's fuzzy texture by concealing the insect in a tiny nylon sleeve. When a nylon sleeve containing a moth was put into the web, the spider wrapped it as she would have wrapped a cricket or grasshopper. Dr. Robinson had his answer. Touch was the clue. The experiment showed that the spider feels the difference between grasshoppers, which have a hard, smooth surface, and moths, which are soft and fuzzy. But touch may be only a partial answer. Odor cannot be ruled out. The spider may be able to detect differences in odor through her feet. But it will take another experiment to find out whether this is the case. Many times in science one experiment raises new questions that can be answered only by other experiments. This chain reaction of questions and experiments enables scientists to reach into the unknown for new information about our world.

To us, the spider's ability to tell the difference between kinds of prey may seem insignificant. But such seemingly small advantages can determine whether or not an animal will survive. Thus evolution is said to "select" certain individuals of a species for long-term survival. Within any species of animals, some individuals can hunt and protect themselves more successfully than others. Those individuals that are best equipped for survival tend to reproduce their own kind, eventually displacing the weaker ones. Over long periods of time species

Silver-backed spider

can change and improve themselves through this process, which biologists call "natural selection."

The theory of natural selection, which is so basic to biology today, was unknown little more than a century ago when Charles Darwin signed on as an unpaid naturalist aboard a sailing expedition. As naturalist on the *Beagle,* a British naval ship sent on a five-year voyage to explore the coast of South America, Darwin's job was to observe and collect plants, animals, and rocks. One of the places the ship stopped at was Brazil. Stepping into the Amazon rain forest for the first time, Darwin was dazzled by the lush variety of plants and the animals so different from those of his native England. The more closely he observed the forest the more aware he became of an intense struggle among tropical plants to reach a place in the sun. This observation gave Darwin an idea—an idea fundamental to modern biology—the struggle for survival. Wherever the ship stopped Darwin began to see animals and plants in a different way. In all kinds of habitats he detected signs of struggle for the necessities of life. He filled many notebooks with observations, drawings, and ideas, and he collected thousands of samples. For years after the *Beagle*'s voyage ended Darwin continued his work. He studied geology and looked at fossils, traces of animals embedded in rock. By comparing the fossils with specimens of plants and animals from his own day, Darwin could trace a kind of family tree linking modern species with those that lived millions of years ago. Yet during all that time changes had occurred within species, in shape or size or color or texture. Certain muscles had enlarged, for example; others had disappeared. As

Darwin tried to understand how these variations had taken place, he returned again and again to the idea of struggle for existence.

Involved in such a struggle, certain individuals were better equipped to survive than others. Darwin saw the situation as one in which nature appeared to "select" those individuals that successfully adapted to their environments.

In 1859 Darwin published his theories in a book, *On the Origin of Species by Means of Natural Selection.* Evolution was not a new idea, but Darwin was the first to present a convincing body of evidence to support it. He was also the first to explain how evolution works. To Darwin, evolution was guided by natural selection.

Modern species are the outcome of hundreds of thousands of years of evolution.

At one time in the history of silver-backed spiders perhaps only a few individuals could discriminate between moths and grasshoppers. But these few had a survival advantage over the spiders that couldn't tell the difference. Because they were better hunters and thus better fed, the discriminators would have been more likely to reach adulthood and to produce other silver-backed spiders like themselves. Of course, evolution has not stopped with the silver-backed spider or with any other species, including ourselves.

Inside a tropical forest you are more aware than in other habitats that evolution is going on twenty-four hours a day. The great variety of ways in which animals obtain food and protect themselves is a constant reminder that very small changes can give an animal immense survival advantages.

Plants
Are
Not
Passive

5

Just as animals have many survival techniques, so plants have also evolved devices for protecting themselves. Plants actively defend themselves and, in some cases, act as predators. Anyone who has ever bitten into a green fruit or picked a rose from a bush or stumbled over a cactus is acquainted with the three principal weapons in the plant arsenal: thorns, spines, and chemical substances that make green fruit distasteful. A bitter taste and a bloody finger may not be the best ways to learn about plant defenses but they are experiences familiar to many inhabitants of the temperate zone.

From desert sands to rose garden, plants all over the world defend themselves. But the greatest variety of plant defenses exists in places having the greatest variety of plants—tropical forests.

Chemical substances such as tannins are the most common vegetable defense. Just as predators avoid bitter-tasting animals, so they avoid bitter-tasting green fruits. The survival of any plant species depends on the production of mature seeds from which new plants can eventually sprout. Young seeds are housed in fruit. As fruit ripens it nourishes the developing seeds inside. If unripe fruits are eaten, the seeds do not have a chance to mature. By making many unripe fruits unpalatable, certain chemicals serve to protect the fruit until it ripens and its seeds mature.

If the vegetation inside a tropical forest had not evolved defenses along with the animals, the forest would probably be extinct today. The thousands of creatures that feed on leaves, fruits, and seeds could have eaten the forest to death. But this calamity did not happen because the vegetation adapted to both its own need for survival and the animals' need for food. Enough food is produced for all the forest vegetarians and, at the same time, enough fruit is protected to ensure the development of seeds.

We don't usually think of trees as active forms of life. Trees stand still and seem to do nothing. But even though a tree is rooted in one place, it can defend itself.

To protect both their foliage and fruit, many trees and plants grow razor-sharp thorns and spines on their trunks. These spines discourage animals that might climb up from the ground to pick fruit before it ripens. Such a climb, as some adventurous botanists have learned, is filled with prickly hazards. Before going up into the canopy to collect a beautiful epiphyte, you always ask whether the prize will be worth the stabs and jabs of hundreds of spines.

By protecting their fruit and foliage from climbing animals, trees save it for canopy dwellers such as birds and monkeys. Canopy animals seem to prefer ripe fruit. Thus spines benefit both the vegetation itself and the canopy animals.

Palms are among the prickliest trees in a tropical forest. They are also the most familiar to people who live in the temperate zone. Any tourist shop in a tropical port sells the all-purpose postcard that shows a coconut palm arched gracefully over a curving shoreline. Coconuts, however, are only one of more than a thousand species of palms. From the tropical forests of Africa to the boulevards of Hollywood, palm trees can be found. Oil palms are particularly important to the economies of several African states.

Some palm species that grow in tropical forests drip with spines. On Barro Colorado Island the long, thin leaflets of a bactris palm are deceivingly delicate. Most palms have no branches—only long, curved leaves called fronds that are divided into leaflets. The tops of the bactris palm's fronds are smooth and green. But underneath, thousands of spines hang like suspended green needles. When walking through

Frond of bactris palm

the forest you learn not to use your bare arm to brush aside this vegetation.

Another species of palm, the black palm, defends itself with spines. From the ground all the way up to the fronds, fearsome-looking spines ring the trunk. High in the canopy the black palm produces cone-shaped clusters of reddish orange fruit. When ripe, this fruit is consumed by monkeys. Uneaten fruit eventually falls to the ground, where dwellers in the lower forest, including a few human explorers, feed on it. The small, round fruit tastes somewhat like a bitter tangerine.

Xylosma trees have their own type of spiny defense. Small clusters of spines called branch spines jut out from the tree's trunk. Like the black palm, the xylosma tree discourages climbers.

Many other kinds of tropical forest trees and shrubs grow spines. They range in shape from the long, slender spines of the black palm to the shorter spines that curve downward like ingrown toenails. Some lianas also have spines and thorns. Rattans, the Asian lianas used for weaving baskets and wicker furniture, have thorny stems. After spending a few hours observing these thorns and spines, you rea-

Black palm

lize that tropical vegetation is certainly ready to ward off attackers.

Although spines and thorns are the most visible means of a plant's protection, it may also have other ways of defending itself that are less obvious. For example, should an animal have a tough enough hide to get past the spines, it might still be in for a surprise. Some fruits are covered with tiny hairs that cause itching and burning.

The sandbox tree spurts out a poisonous sap if its bark is cut. This tree also has a unique method of dispersing its seeds. When the fruit ripens, it explodes with a loud noise. Like tiny flying missiles, the flat, round, coin-like seeds are scattered in all directions, up to eighty feet away from the tree. During the eighteenth century, long before the invention of ball-point pens, the unexploded fruits of this tree were used to hold sand that was sprinkled on letters to blot the ink. From the use of its fruit as a container for sand, the sandbox tree got its popular name.

Plants not only defend themselves, some also eat meat. Several species of carnivorous plants grow in the rain forests of both the Old and the New World.

In the swamp forests of Brazil, Cuba, and the Guianas grow bladderworts, whose lacy, divided leaves have small bladders. These plants feed on water spiders, small roundworms, and other tiny water creatures.

Another more commonly found carnivorous plant has leaf tips which broaden into pitcher-shaped leaves. The pitcher plant, as it is popularly called, attracts prey with a chemical secretion. Drawn

Bladderwort

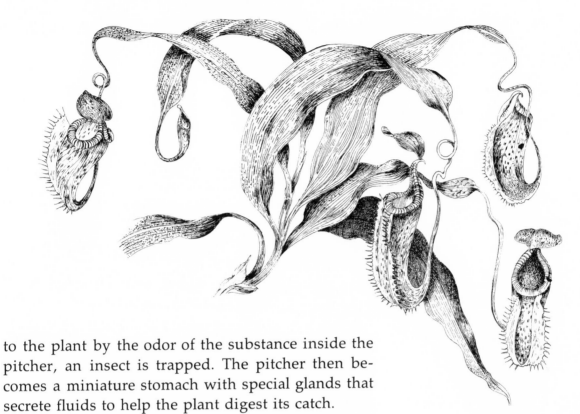

Pitcher plant

to the plant by the odor of the substance inside the pitcher, an insect is trapped. The pitcher then becomes a miniature stomach with special glands that secrete fluids to help the plant digest its catch.

Like many forms of life in a tropical forest, certain carnivorous plants share a relationship with other creatures. One species of spiders lives inside the pitchers. Instead of devouring these spiders, the pitcher plants, for some unknown reason, provide a home for them. The spiders also benefit in another way. They depend on the plants for their food. Some of the insects attracted by the pitcher plants are eaten by the spiders.

Predators of some creatures, pitcher plants are the protectors of others. In a tropical forest, where nothing is quite what it seems, the relationship between pitcher plants and spiders is only one of many surprising interactions.

One of the most unusual and incompletely understood interactions involves certain kinds of tropical plants and ants. An entire group of plants are known as "ant plants" because they are inhabited by ants. For more than a hundred years scientists have known about these ant-plant associations, but they do not know why they exist only in the tropics. Curiously, each species of ant plant is home for only one species of ants, and these ants live nowhere else. Hollow twigs and leaves and swollen stalks provide homes for entire ant colonies.

The ants obviously benefit from the association by using the plant for both food and shelter. But what about the plant? Does it also benefit?

In some cases, such as the bullhorn acacia of Central America, scientists have discovered a cooperative relationship between plant and ant. Living in the large, paired, hornlike thorns that give the bullhorn acacia its name, ants feed on sugar produced by nectar glands on the leaf stalks and on tiny beads of protein that grow on the tips of leaflets. The bullhorn acacia benefits from its ants in two ways. First, the ants drive away insects and other vegetarians that would eat the tree's foliage. Second, the ants protect their host tree from vines and strangler-type plants by biting off the tendrils of any plant growing in the area other than their own.

No one knows just how many ant-plant relationships are mutually beneficial. Perhaps future scientists will learn the answer. In the meantime, the interaction between ants and bullhorn acacias demonstrates that cooperation as a survival technique is not exclusive among animals. Plants *and* animals also share cooperative relationships.

Bullhorn acacia

Action at Ground Level: Ants and More Ants

Interactions occur at every level of a tropical forest from the ground to the canopy. As we have seen, the basic interaction between the sun and green plants is the battery that powers the entire forest system. And within that system are many other relationships between animals of different species, between members of the same species, and between animals and their environment. Without such relationships among animals and plants, life in any forest ecosystem would be impossible. But in

6

a tropical forest, with its great diversity of life and intense competition for food and space, the interactions are more subtle and intricate than in other forests. At a time when coexistence among different human societies is so important to our survival, scientists are paying particular attention to the techniques which have enabled thousands of different species to live together in tropical forests for millions of years.

Just as people use their habitats for a variety of purposes, so other animals use their living space for different activities. Within each level of the forest, creatures hunt for food, mate, bear young, defend themselves against their enemies, and communicate with other members of their species. In the process of living, all animals, including people, change their environments in some way. Man's alterations are often on a large scale. We dam rivers, tunnel through mountains, build canals, fill swamps, and cut down entire forests. Our present standard of living was made possible by the Industrial Revolution, but we *are* paying a price for it. Some of the things we have done have endangered the balance of life on our planet. Our air is polluted, oil slicks threaten marine life, chemicals like mercury are dumped into the oceans where they pass through food chains, some animals have become extinct, and one of our major lakes, Lake Erie, is dead.

Other animals change their environment on a smaller scale. Rarely do they threaten the natural processes of rebirth and regrowth. The dams built by beavers, the tunnels of moles, the holes made in trees by woodpeckers do not harm the environment by upsetting the ecological balance.

If you look closely at the ground level of a tropical forest, you can see how one group of creatures changes the environment. Tiny trails and mounds are evidence of the engineering skill of the largest group of insects in the tropics—ants; hundreds of millions of them crawl in monotonous processions along the forest floor. On your first visit to a tropical forest you are aware of ants everywhere: on the ground, on plants, on tree trunks and fruits and flowers and branches—everywhere. But the varieties on the forest floor are particularly evident at each step you take. At first they all look alike, but you soon learn that ant species differ as much from each other as do people. Ants come in different colors—red, black, and brown—and in different sizes. Some sting, some bite, some eat foliage, and some eat other insects.

The species that makes the most noticeable changes in its habitat is the leaf-cutting ant. Societies of these ants range over the lowest levels of the forest. The area near a leaf cutter's nest is easy to spot because it is so bare. There are neither small plants nor underbrush. Some tiny trees near the nest will have no leaves. The leaves remaining on other trees in the area look as if they have been cut out by a child making paper dolls. A bare area and cutout leaves are sure signs of the presence of leaf-cutting ants, one of the most numerous and important plant-using insects in New World tropical forests.

Leaf cutters live in the basement of the forest. About twelve feet below the tree roots a colony of several million individuals digs its underground cavities. Like workers who dig a large hole for the foundation of a building, the leaf cutters must trans-

Leaf-cutting ant

port the dirt somewhere. This soil is brought to the surface. Because the soil beneath a tropical forest floor is barren, this excavated dirt contains no nutrients to support new plant growth.

Within their underground habitat leaf-cutting ants cultivate an unusual crop—fungus. To human farmers, fungi mean disease. Entire wheat fields have been killed by wheat rust, a disease caused by a fungus. But for leaf cutters, the farmers of the forest floor, fungus is the main food crop, eaten by both young and mature ants. Whenever a young female ant leaves the colony to start a new nest, she carries a mouthful of fungus with her.

The fungus cultivated by leaf cutters is of particular interest to biologists. There are many fungi in a tropical forest. Some cause diseases in plants and animals, including man, but the leaf cutters' fungus lives on dead leaves and does not infect anything.

Any farmer needs to fertilize his crops, and leaf cutters are no exception. To enrich their fungus gardens, these ants use particles of leaves. Each day patrols of worker ants crawl to the surface to collect the leaves. Marking their trails with an invisible chemical secreted by glands in their bodies, the ants leave a scent which they use to find their way back to the nest. No other creature but man can erase the trail. Many other forest species, particularly those with poor eyesight, mark their trails with a body scent. Looking down at the ground, you can see the leaf cutters' trails radiating like tiny highways from their nests. Acting as a highway maintenance crew, the ants continually clear and repair these trails.

As worker ants move along branches, they use

their scissor-like jaws with surgical precision to cut tiny semicircles out of the leaves. Because the ants cut all the leaves from the shrubs near their nest, these plants eventually die, leaving a conspicuous bare area that makes the nest easy to locate. But the ants do not confine their leaf gathering to the area near their nest. They are known to travel as far as a hundred yards to collect leaves from the crowns of trees that rise forty feet or more above the ground. Leaf cutters seem to spread out their foraging in such a way that the trees do not suffer the same stripping as the shrubs in the immediate vicinity of the nest.

Every day columns of leaf cutters gather leaf particles and transport them back to the nest. Each ant carries in its mouth a leaf particle often larger than its own body. Like a slow-moving parade of tiny green sails, the ants sense their way back to the nest. Top-heavy and mouths full, they are easy targets for parasitic flies that hover overhead, waiting to lay their eggs on ants' bodies. But the leaf cutters are prepared. Hitchhiking on the leaf particles are smaller worker ants—mini-workers—who act as tail gunners. Their sharp pincers aimed upward, the mini-workers snap at approaching flies, frightening them away.

Leaf-cutting ants
forage for food.

Back inside their underground nest, the ants chew up the leaves to make a mulch, a manure-like spread used as fertilizer for the fungus.

Like other organized societies, including our own, leaf-cutting ants have a garbage-disposal problem. Some remove dead ants and wastes to an underground dumping area. On Barro Colorado the leaf cutters have a trash dump on top of the ground, and one colony deposits its wastes in a stream. If the wastes remained in the stream, like man's sewage they could cause pollution. But inside the forest sewage is recycled. Rich in nutrients, the leaf cutters' trash dumps are rapidly invaded by tree roots, which remove the nutrients for their own leaves.

From plant to ant to fungus to ant and back to tree roots, the nutrients of the forest are used and recycled—another example of the efficient use of energy that helps to make a tropical forest a stable ecosystem.

Leaf-cutting ants are found from Louisiana south to Argentina. Outside the forest, in farming areas, they are pests, stripping leaves from crops and causing farmers to shift crops to different fields. Inside the forest the ants live in balance with the other animal populations and do not endanger vegetation.

The leaf-cutting ants have been studied for more than a hundred years, but scientists still feel that they know very little about these creatures and how they affect their environment.

Sharing the forest floor with leaf-cutting ants are a completely different subfamily of ants—the army ants. A complex set of relationships exists among army ants and the many different creatures that make up a band of camp followers.

There are several species of army ants but they are all meat-eaters, carnivores. Unlike the vegetarian leaf cutters, who use their mandibles to cut their food, army ants pinch their prey with their mandibles. Descended from wasps, army ants sting and bite their victims. Although they may also sting and bite people and other vertebrates, army ants feed largely on arthropods, a large group of invertebrates that includes spiders and insects such as grasshoppers, roaches, and crickets. Of course these insects try to camouflage themselves beneath fallen leaves, but raiding squadrons of hungry ants flush them from their hiding places.

Every day the forest floor is the scene of fierce struggles within the insect world. By bending close to the ground you can watch army ants as they forage. Moving in columns four to eight ants abreast or in swarms thousands of ants wide, the ants come in seemingly endless numbers. They move quickly, over logs, leaves, the petals of fallen blossoms. Invisible and odorless to humans, the scent each ant leaves marks the trail for other ants. The area in the path of the marching ants swarms with the frenzied activity of insects flying up from their leafy covers. Parasitic flies buzz and hover nearby, waiting to lay their eggs on the bodies of fleeing insects.

Perched in surrounding shrubs, ant-following birds—so-called because they travel with army ants —call softly to one another. These birds, of which there are more than fifty different species, do not eat army ants, but they depend for almost all of their food supply on insects that the ants flush up from the forest floor.

Ornithologists, biologists who study birds, can track the movements of ant-following birds. On

Barro Colorado, Dr. Yoshika Oniki and Dr. Edwin Willis have studied such birds for several years. One of their principal tools is a mist net, an almost invisible nylon net used to collect birds without injuring them.

The mist net that ornithologists use today is an updated version of a net developed hundreds of years ago by the Japanese for the purpose of capturing birds for food. A scientist today stretches and secures the net between two trees. Because ant-following birds live in the lower level of the forest, it is easy to catch them. The net is hung above the ants' foraging route, a route that the ant-following birds will also take. When a bird flies into the net, it is held gently.

Scientists like Dr. Oniki and Dr. Willis capture birds in order to obtain certain information and to mark them. Each bird is weighed and its wing length measured. An ornithologist keeps careful notes, recording these figures along with the age of the bird and information about whether it is molting, shedding its feathers. Then he marks the bird by placing four colored plastic bands around its legs, two bands on each leg. Each bird has its own unique color combination that serves as an identification bracelet. The colored bands can be easily spotted through binoculars. Whenever a banded bird is sighted, an ornithologist need only refer to his notebook to learn how long ago and where the bird was captured.

Bird-watching scientists learn to be patient and quiet. In the late afternoon or evening Dr. Oniki and Dr. Willis go into the forest to check the movement of the army ants that the birds accompany. If the colony is on the move, the ants will be setting up a new bivouac, a kind of temporary nest, for the night. The scientists need to locate the bivouac because they will return here in the morning. The next day they get out of bed around dawn in order to be inside the forest by seven o'clock. They pack sandwiches for lunch and carry a mist net, small scales to weigh birds, a thermometer to check temperatures, and plastic raincoats in case it rains. To avoid mosquito bites, they wear long-sleeved shirts, long pants, and lace-up boots with socks. They pull up the socks on the outside of their trousers so as not to be bothered by the stings and bites of the army ants.

When the light reaches the dark lower levels of the forest, the ants begin to move. Staying ten or fifteen yards behind the raid, Dr. Oniki and Dr. Willis listen for the calls of the spotted ant bird, the barred woodcreeper, or other species of ant-following birds. With binoculars the ornithologists scan the dim forest interior. Ant-following birds are difficult to see because their dark feathers blend with the browns near the forest floor.

The ants advance, moving about fifteen yards an hour. Dr. Willis and Dr. Oniki also move slowly, to keep the birds in sight without alarming them. They may spend fifteen minutes or all day studying the birds—counting how many of each species are sighted, noting what time each bird arrives and departs, observing their foraging, feuding, courtship, and other behavior. If there are unbanded birds, the scientists wait for them to become accustomed to their presence and then set up a mist net.

During a day Dr. Willis and Dr. Oniki may walk several miles listening for the calls of ant-following

Spotted ant birds

birds and watching the ground for ant columns. At the end of the day they use their notes to plot a bird's movement on a map of Barro Colorado. Each time the same bird is observed a dot is put on the map to indicate where it was seen. When many sightings have been made, the dots can be connected to give a picture of an ant-following bird's travels over the island. Dr. Willis has kept track of some ant-following birds for more than ten years.

From their studies, he and Dr. Oniki have learned that the birds will leave their own territory to follow ants into other parts of the forest, even if this means trespassing on the domains of other ant-following birds. Ordinarily, birds stay within their own territories and drive out intruders, but ant-following birds seem to be more tolerant of trespassers. Also the study shows that the number of ant-following birds on Barro Colorado is declining. One reason is that ant-following birds from the mainland forest will not leave their cool, shaded habitats to fly through the hot, sunlit sky across the Panama Canal and start new colonies on Barro Colorado Island. The other reason is one sadly recognized by scientists. On islands and in special nature reserves—both of which are isolated, self-contained communities—the animals start dying out. Scientists have even figured out a mathematical rule to describe the process: dividing an area by ten divides the number of animals in the original area by two. Animals that survive in one environment often cannot recolonize another even though the two environments may be similar and close to each other. In the Amazon forest, for example, Dr. Oniki and Dr. Willis have found that many of the ant-following birds on the south side of the lower Amazon are different from the ones on the north side. In terms of survival, this means that certain species would be threatened with extinction should their habitats be destroyed because they might not be able to survive on the opposite bank of the river and would not fly across to start new colonies. As people continue to spread over the face of the earth, pushing animals into parks and reserves, one can only wonder about the future survival of the many rare species that now live in tropical forests.

Birds are not the only creatures that follow army ants. More than two hundred species of tiny scavenger flies also depend on army ants for their food supply. Active in the dumps where army ants deposit their litter, scavenger flies feed on the remains of insects killed by the ants and on dead army ants.

More than followers, a group of small beetles actually live with colonies of army ants and ride on the ants. Instead of eating these beetles, army ants accept them in spite of the fact that the beetles prey on the ants' young. Dr. Roger Akre, an entomologist from Washington State University, has spent much time observing the interactions between these small creatures. He has learned that the beetles clean or groom the army-ant soldiers and workers. The grooming acts like a tranquilizer, calming the ants. At times, ants and beetles groom each other. The beetles benefit from the relationship by having a continuous food supply of ant larvae as well as leftovers from the ants' foraging. In addition, the ants protect the beetles from other predators.

Mimicry is also involved in this intricate relationship. Except to a trained eye some beetles are

Look-alike beetle
and army ant

almost indistinguishable from army ants. Not only do the beetles look like army ants, they also have the same smell. By rubbing against the bodies of army ants, beetles transfer ant odor to themselves. This makes it easier for beetles to become part of an army-ant colony.

At least two methods of survival, cooperation and camouflage, characterize the interaction between army ants and beetles. Although small, these creatures of the forest floor interact in ways that might be instructive to master intelligence agents.

Life in an army-ant colony follows a highly organized pattern. For a certain number of days the colony, which consists of a queen, soldiers, workers, and young, moves each night. This marching period is followed by a stationary period, a time when the colony nests in the same location for several weeks.

Birds follow only a few of the many species of army ants; only those species that form wide armies or swarms on the ground flush insects for the birds. These species, called "swarm raiders," march more than a hundred yards every day for eleven to seventeen days. During this time they set up a bivouac in a different place each night. The army-ant bivouac is an amazing construction consisting only of ants. Locking their long legs together, the ants form layers and layers of wiggling, breathing bodies, clinging together in a dense mass. Usually the bivouac is attached to the side of a log or to the lower part of a tree trunk. From a distance the bivouac appears to be a swelling on the trunk. Close up, it heaves with the movement of thousands of legs. In the center of this mass of life is the queen ant.

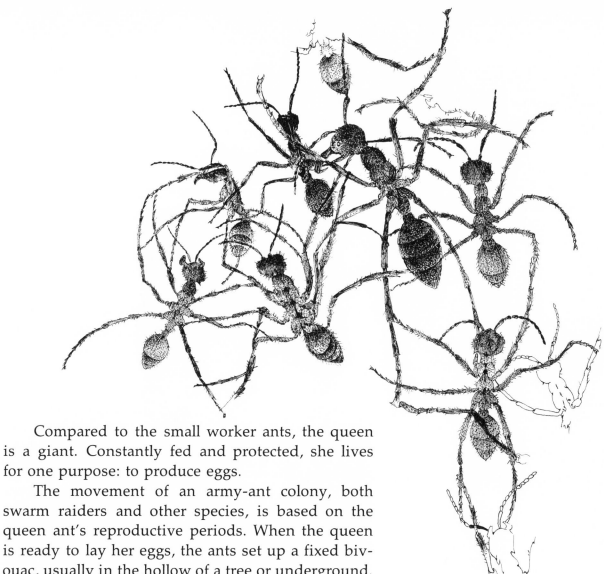

Compared to the small worker ants, the queen is a giant. Constantly fed and protected, she lives for one purpose: to produce eggs.

The movement of an army-ant colony, both swarm raiders and other species, is based on the queen ant's reproductive periods. When the queen is ready to lay her eggs, the ants set up a fixed bivouac, usually in the hollow of a tree or underground. Here they live for the next nineteen to twenty-two days, while the queen lays almost 250,000 eggs. During this time the eggs hatch. After the new worker ants come out of their cocoons, the colony leaves its stationary nest and resumes its daily marches.

The number of eggs produced by the queen is

Small part of an
army-ant bivouac

enormous. Like most other insects, army ants over-produce. Because many army ants are killed in the raids, a large number of new worker ants is needed to keep the colony going.

New World army ants are one of the major predators of the forest floor. Some scientists believe that army ants are one of the few controls on social insects, such as other kinds of ants and some wasps, in the tropics. Yet the survival of thousands of other creatures—birds, beetles, and scavenger flies—depends on army ants.

Army ants are found as far north as California, Ohio, and North Carolina, but the northern species raid underground or at night and do not attract birds. Some northern birds that migrate south for the winter, such as Swainson's thrushes and hooded warblers, do follow army ants in the tropical forest.

In Africa's tropical forests are found driver ants, the Old World relatives of army ants. Far more dangerous than army ants, driver ants are said to be capable of attacking and killing huge pythons and of cutting and carrying away other vertebrates that are trapped. But like their relatives, driver ants share relationships with various kinds of birds, including thrushes. The largest number of ant-following birds, however, are in the American tropics. As in the New World, there are no ant-bird relationships in the temperate zones of Old World forests and none in the temperate forests of Asia and Australia.

In the tropical forest system army and driver ants fill a complex niche. Social insects, they live in highly organized groups. Carnivores, population-control agents, providers—army and driver ants play all of these roles, demonstrating how closely the survival of one forest species is linked to another.

Crawling, Slithering Creatures: Reptiles and Amphibians

7

Among the many animals that follow army ants to feed on fleeing insects are an occasional lizard, such as the racerunner, and some big toads. Lizards and toads belong to two large groups of cold-blooded animals that are as fascinating to scientists as to the rest of us. Lizards are members of the reptile family, which also includes snakes. Toads and frogs are amphibians, animals which usually hatch in water and live there when young, breathing with gills, but which, as adults, can live on land, for they breathe with lungs. The body temperature of amphibians and reptiles is not regulated within the animal's body, as is the case for people, dogs, and monkeys. Instead a cold-blooded animal's temperature varies with its behavior and its environment. Because of the constant warmth and high humidity, a tropical forest provides ideal conditions for many cold-blooded animals, and they are found there in great numbers.

Different species of amphibians and reptiles are distributed through all levels of the forest—at the edges of streams and ponds, along river banks, and in the trees of the canopy. Depending on their habitat, whether dark forest floor or green foliage high above ground, these animals are as masterfully camouflaged as leaf-mimicking insects. You have to be extraordinarily observant to find a turtle on the forest floor or to tell the difference between floating logs and crocodiles. Some animals, however, such as the poison-arrow frogs of South America, wear strikingly brilliant warning coloration. Feeding on plants, insects, birds, rodents, and each other, the cold-blooded animals participate in a variety of food chains.

Of all these creatures, snakes come most easily to mind when we think of tropical forests. Partly this is because we have been brainwashed by "jungle" stories and movies. Many species of snakes live in Old and New World forests, but few are as deadly as those in the movies, and they do not slither and coil menacingly from every vine and branch. It is possible to walk through a tropical forest for several days without seeing a snake. This is not to deny the existence of poisonous tropical snakes. There are some—the venomous South American bushmasters, the same family to which our rattlesnake belongs, and the Gaboon viper of Africa, one of the deadliest snakes of the forest floor. Its venom paralyzes prey and can be fatal to man, but the chance of being bitten is rare, for this snake can hardly be provoked, even to defend itself.

Tropical forests are homes for the largest snakes in the world—the reticulated python of Asia, which can be as long as thirty feet and as heavy as three hundred pounds.

Two of the best-known tropical snakes live in Central and South American forests—boa constrictors and giant anacondas. The boa, although it is sometimes kept as a pet, can also kill a person. The twelve-foot boa kills by coiling around its victims and squeezing them to death. Some boas can kill large prey such as monkeys, but usually they feed on small mammals such as forest-floor rodents. The brilliant green emerald tree boa feeds on birds and monkeys. This and other tree-dwelling snakes have developed keener eyesight than most ground dwellers because they cannot depend on scent to lead them to their prey.

Living near streams and ponds, the twenty-five-foot giant anaconda, second largest snake in the world, waits for animals to come to drink. A strong swimmer, the anaconda drags its prey underwater —and swallows it whole, as do all snakes.

On the forest floor poisonous coral snakes and their harmless mimics sport warning coloration, bold bands of black, red, and yellow that signal predators to stay away. The coral snakes eat lizards and other snakes.

Gaboon viper

Anaconda

Although most tropical snakes are not poisonous, it is a good idea to wear high, solid boots when walking through a tropical forest, not only for protection against possible snakebites but against the more common nuisances—the small ticks, stinging ants, and leeches. To a visitor who goes into a tropical forest clothed from head to foot, it seems impossible that forest tribes can exist with no more than a few leaves girding their loins. But the forest Indians know their territory as intimately as we know our city streets. Although some scientists who know the forest well wear open sandals and shorts, this is not advisable for a newcomer.

For people who live off the forest, such as the Stone Age Tasaday tribe, cave dwellers of the Philippines Mindanao rain forest, tadpoles and frogs are tasty food. You can also find them on the menu of a good French restaurant, but they will not be prepared Tasaday style—wrapped in orchid leaves and roasted on hot coals.

Millions of frogs inhabit tropical forests. Some mimic leaves, some glide, some crawl, some are multicolored, and a few are poisonous. Most are nocturnal, filling the night world with fantastic choruses. At least half of them live in trees, where they have developed very different adaptations from their relatives on the forest floor. Ground frogs hop and jump, fine methods of traveling along the forest floor but hardly suitable for moving through the trees. Some tree frogs, such as the flying frog of Asian forests, have webbed feet which they spread when they want to move about. Actually, flying frogs don't really fly. They jump off a branch and their webbed feet enable them to glide as much as forty feet before landing. Many tree frogs have large disks on their toes which enable them to climb on branches. The little disks stick to surfaces like the rubber suction disks on the ends of certain darts that children shoot from guns. Because tree frogs do more climbing and walking than hopping, their leg muscles are not as fully developed as those of toads, their jumping relatives on the forest floor.

We usually think of frogs laying their eggs in ponds, but a few tree frogs reproduce without benefit of streams or ponds. In tropical American forests some tree frogs lay their eggs in water collected by the bromeliads in the canopy. Others lay their eggs on leaves that hang over streams. When the eggs hatch, the tadpoles fall into the water.

On the forest floor, the enormous number of New World frogs and other amphibians and reptiles have evolved efficient living arrangements. Dr. Martha Crump of the University of Kansas studied these arrangements among sixty-two species of frogs, salamanders, and lizards in an area of Amazon forest near Belém, Brazil. She discovered that these creatures divide or partition their environment in such a way that each species can get the most out of

Tree frog

its habitat. Some species of frogs use the same area of forest floor by day that other species use at night. Some confine themselves to only one small area, while others adapt to larger areas of forest floor. Dr. Crump learned that breeding frogs in particular partition their environment. Some breed in diverse kinds of ponds and swamps—large or small, deep or shallow. Other species breed only in ponds bordered by dense vegetation. The male courting frogs also select special sites for calling to females.

This introduces another problem—one of communication. With so many frogs and other animals creating so much noise, how can a male frog make himself heard by a female of his own species? The problem is similar to that at human parties. How do you carry on a conversation in the midst of so many chattering voices? A Barro Colorado biologist, Dr. A. Stanley Rand, whose specialty is reptiles and amphibians, studies this question by recording frog choruses in Panama and Brazil. He is trying to learn how the frogs manage to communicate against the noisy background of the forest night.

In addition, Dr. Rand has spent several years studying iguanas. Found only in the New World and on Madagascar and the Fiji Islands, iguanas are among the most primitive-looking animals in the tropics. Some resemble miniature dinosaurs, and others look like drawings of fabled sea monsters and dragons. Probably best-known are the marine iguanas of the Galápagos Islands off Ecuador, which were visited by Charles Darwin. Their habitat is a rocky shore, quite different from that of the rain forest species, who live in trees.

For a number of years Dr. Rand has studied the

arboreal iguanas of Barro Colorado Island. Off Barro Colorado is a smaller island, Slothia, that is known to have been a nesting site for female iguanas since the 1930's. Like Barro Colorado, Slothia was also created when the waters of the Panama Canal rose to create Gatun Lake. Usually female iguanas nest by themselves, but those on Barro Colorado swim to the tiny island each February and nest in a group. Dr. Rand believes that they do this to protect their eggs from birds, snakes, and the many other egg-eating predators that live on Barro Colorado. Only vultures follow the iguanas to the small island.

Slothia's beach is not very large, but it can accommodate as many as thirty animals at one time. In order to observe iguanas without disturbing them, Dr. Rand made a blind at the edge of the nesting site. Camouflaged, he could watch the iguanas and take motion pictures of their activity. From the top of the hill on Barro Colorado, he could also watch through binoculars.

When the females first arrive on Slothia, they are swollen with eggs. During their first few days away from their treetop habitat the iguanas dry off from their swim, bask in the sun, and test various nesting sites in the small, sandy clearing. Then they begin to dig the burrows in which they will lay their eggs. Using both front and back feet, an iguana digs with scratching motions of her long claws. She burrows downward at an angle until she has excavated a tunnel about the length of her own body. During the digging she faces the burrow, pushing her snout farther and farther inside. As the tunnel deepens all that can be seen of the iguana is her tail. While digging she is very aggressive and threatens other approaching females by opening her mouth wide and breathing out in a loud huff. If the threat display doesn't work and another female interrupts her digging, she bites the meddlesome creature.

An iguana doesn't dig her nest all at once. She may spend portions of two days working on it, leaving and entering her nest several times. The burrow is complete when it is deep enough and wide enough for the iguana to work completely underground. Then she stops digging and lays her eggs. When she comes out of the nest after laying the eggs, her sides are visibly shrunken and wrinkled. She then begins to seal her nest, using front and back feet to fill up the burrow with the same dirt she recently removed. Using her snout, she tightly packs the dirt. Once she has sealed her nest, she scratches the surrounding earth to disguise its location. Then she leaves, seemingly uninterested in guarding the nest, and begins to fill in other burrows. Sometimes she pushes dirt into the face of another iguana who is still digging or laying eggs. When this happens, the trapped female tries to dig her way out, but occasionally she fails and dies.

Dr. Rand has observed that iguanas sometimes dig into already filled nests, unearthing eggs. Ignored by the iguanas, the unearthed eggs are quickly eaten by the vultures who wait for such accidental feasts.

Unlike animals that regularly nest in colonies, these iguanas do not stand guard over their nests. If a female leaves her nest during egg laying, she does not even fight with another female who moves into it. Dr. Rand believes that the iguanas of Barro Colorado may be in the process of evolving colonial

Arboreal iguana

(group) nesting behavior. Right now, he believes, they are in a primitive stage, developing from solitary nesters to colonial nesters. If this is the case, these iguanas are a living example of evolution at work. The pressure to escape predators has forced them to change their behavior. Colonial nesting is another kind of cooperation among members of the same species—cooperation that gives animals yet another advantage in the struggle for survival.

Tropical
Forest
Birds

8

The study of birds brings many scientists to tropical forests. It is not difficult to understand why. More different species of birds live in the tropics than anyplace else on earth. In one small area of the Amazon forest near Belém, Brazil, more than 450 species have been counted.

In addition to birds that live in tropical forests all year round, there are also visitors. A crossroads between the Northern and Southern hemispheres, Brazil's tropical forest lies in the pathway of migrating birds. Many of these birds remain in tropical forests during the temperate zone's winter.

Just as frogs partition their environment, so do the hundreds of species of tropical birds. Although some birds range throughout their up-and-down world, most species can be placed in one of four general groups: ground birds, low forest birds, upper forest birds, and canopy birds.

As their name suggests, ground birds live close to the forest floor. Tinamous, ground doves, and some ant-following birds belong to this group. Low forest birds live and forage in between ground and canopy. Upper forest birds live in the lowest layer of the canopy and forage inside the forest. Canopy birds live in the tops of the tallest trees. Above them is the open sky. For these birds, the top section of the canopy is the ground floor. They may nest in one of the towering trees whose crown breaks through the canopy and rises above it. Canopy birds rarely penetrate into the dim forest below. Theirs is a world of bright sunlight and tropical breezes.

One's first impression of tropical birds is color —the vivid blues, yellows, greens, and reds of hummingbirds, parakeets, parrots, and toucans. Although beautiful to a human eye, a bird's coloration is more than mere decoration that brightens up the forest. Among birds, coloration can camouflage and it can communicate.

Male birds are the more colorful sex. In some species the male bird's colors become more brilliant during the mating season. By showing his colors, a male bird signals his interest in female birds. Ruffled feathers may also be a part of mating displays.

As camouflage, bright coloration helps a bird

Four tropical birds
(top to bottom):
a hummingbird,
toucan,
parrot (left)
and parakeet

to blend with the equally colorful blossoms of tropical forest vegetation. In some cases bright colors may attract insects who mistake a bird for a blossom. Instead of finding nectar, those insects find themselves on the way to a bird's stomach.

The duller coloration of female birds serves a protective purpose. While nesting, a female bird blends into the dull grays and browns of her nest. A brighter color would make her an easy target for predators.

Birds use sound as well as color to communicate. For many centuries poets have written about the songs of birds. In recent years scientists have learned that there is more to a bird's call than music.

Birds everywhere communicate with calls, but the sounds they make seem to be particularly varied and complex in the tropics. Bird calls are used to communicate with mates, young birds, rivals, companions, and even with enemies. Each species has its own set of signals, some of which are repeated in the rhythmic, musical patterns we call songs. By observing the behavior of birds in the wild and by recording and analyzing their calls, scientists such as Dr. Peter Marler of Rockefeller University are able to determine what certain songs communicate to other birds.

Most species have an alarm cry signaling danger to other birds. The cry may be loud and piercing or it may be soft. Its purpose is to warn other birds and to threaten the intruding predator. When a young bird has been caught by a predator, the alarm cry is a call for help.

Different calls play a part in courtship and mating. Male birds of certain species sing long and, to the human ear, beautiful songs to attract females. If she is attracted, a female bird responds with a song of her own.

Other calls are used when a bird finds food. Food-finding calls summon a group of birds together for a meal.

A nesting female sings a different song from that of two rival males. A young bird that has strayed from its nest makes a distinctive sound that its mother can use to locate it.

The different calls that birds make are a language, a language without words. Often hidden from sight in the treetops, birds use their nonverbal language to signal other birds many yards away. These elaborate vocal calls probably evolved as a means of surviving in an environment dark and curtained with foliage. For a bird inside a forest, its song is an advantage, enabling it to communicate while remaining in the protective cover of leaves and blossoms.

Besides communicating by songs and coloration, birds use odors and, where they are close enough to see each other, head and feather movements. Trapped birds may give off a strong odor or squirt a horrible-smelling oil from their mouths. By raising its feathers a bird can suddenly take on the appearance of a large, furry animal. This kind of startle display is used to frighten predators. Other head and feather movements are used by courting males to attract females. Some of the most spectacular courting displays are those of male birds of paradise, who live in various Old World tropical forests.

Birds seek to protect themselves not only through startle displays, alarm cries, and camouflage but through banding together in groups. Two or more species may get together, forming what scientists call a "mixed-species flock," another example of cooperation as a survival technique. Birds all over the world form mixed-species flocks, but these groups exist in greater numbers and greater variety in a tropical forest.

Dr. Martin Moynihan, director of the Smithsonian Tropical Research Institute, made a special study of such flocks in Panama. To Dr. Moynihan, they are another example of the complex interactions that take place among different species in tropical habitats. Learning more about the roles of the various species in a mixed flock helps us to understand how nonhuman animals organize their societies.

On Barro Colorado Island one of the most commonly observed mixed-species flocks consists of blue tanagers, green tanagers, plain-colored tanagers, and honeycreepers. With the exception of the plain-colored tanager, who is named for its dull, gray color, these are small, brilliantly colored birds.

Blue and green tanager and honeycreeper flocks are found almost throughout lowland Panama in habitats at the edge of the forest. The birds that make up these flocks live in the upper canopy and never descend very far below the treetops. They eat fruit, nectar, and insects.

Within a mixed flock, each species has a special role. In the blue and green tanager and honeycreeper group one species is central, the one around which the other species flock. Dr. Moynihan learned that the plain-colored tanagers play this central role. Restless, noisy creatures, these particular birds attract others. Yet they do not actively join other birds,

Blue tanager

Summer tanager

Golden-masked tanager

Plain-colored tanager

Bananaquit

nor do they threaten them. In fact, it may be that other birds join plain-colored tanagers *because* of their dull coloration. Dr. Moynihan suggests that this coloration is neutral, unlikely to frighten or repel potential companions.

The palm tanager, another member of the blue and green tanager and honeycreeper flock, also attracts other species. But unlike plain-colored tanagers, palm tanagers also join and follow other birds. And although the palm tanager attracts other birds to the flock, it is not the central species around which the entire flock organizes.

The other members of this tanager and honeycreeper flock—blue tanagers, golden-masked tana-

Five members of the blue
and green tanager
and honeycreeper flock

gers, and green honeycreepers—are mostly joiners.

One member, the summer tanager, is a migrant. During the temperate zone's winter months, the summer tanager remains with the mixed flock.

Bananaquits, who join or follow other birds, have a special effect on the tanager and honeycreeper flock during the mating season. At this time, male bananaquits sing noisily. The mating calls of the males attract not only female bananaquits but also other birds, particularly green honeycreepers.

The attraction that one species has for another holds the flock together and enables it to function as a social group. Scientists like Dr. Moynihan, who are trying to learn why tropical forest animals have survived successfully for such a long time, find that a mixed-species flock offers birds at least two advantages in the struggle for survival. The mixed flock increases the ability of each individual species to protect its members against predators and to locate food. The old notion of "safety in numbers" is correct: predators are far less likely to attack a large group of birds than a small flock. A larger flock has more birds to spot a predator and warn the others. And foraging as a group, mixed-species flocks find more food than single-species flocks, simply because there are more different kinds of birds searching for a variety of food.

Mixed-species flocks are one example of cooperation among different species of birds. Another occurs between two groups of birds that live in the mid-canopy layer, oropendolas and caciques, and a most unlikely ally—a parasite, the giant cowbird. Rather than build a nest of her own, the female giant cowbird lays her eggs in nests made by oropendolas and caciques. Oddly enough, in some cases these birds accept the giant cowbird's eggs. Usually a parasite is bad, a creature to be avoided, but not in this instance.

This intricate relationship was discovered by Dr. Neal Griffith Smith of the Smithsonian Tropical Research Institute, who studied the habits of oropendolas and caciques throughout Panama and the Canal Zone. His observations took him at least sixty feet into the canopy, where these birds build their bag-like nests during the dry season. Standing in the basket of an elevator-like crane popularly known as a "cherry picker," Dr. Smith could reach out and collect nests to take back to his laboratory.

Often some fifty or sixty nests are constructed in one tree, housing an entire colony of birds. And it is not unusual for the birds to return to the same tree year after year. Dr. Smith knows of a site in the Canal Zone that has been used for over thirty years.

While conducting his study, Dr. Smith became skillful at returning nests to their sites in the trees. A resourceful scientist, he found that an ordinary rat-trap was a dandy gadget for reattaching a nest to a limb.

The more he observed oropendolas and caciques, the more aware he became of their unusual nest-building habits and their close relationships with predators and with other creatures sharing the same habitat. The chief predator of oropendolas and caciques is a group of botflies. These insects are para-sites that lay their eggs or deposit their larvae on young oropendola and cacique chicks. When large numbers of larvae burrow into a chick's body, they can eventually destroy it.

(From top to bottom)
Cacique, oropendola,
and giant cowbird

Examining more than a thousand oropendola and cacique nests, Dr. Smith discovered that some of these birds protect themselves from botflies by building nests in the same trees as wasps and stingless but biting bees. Again using a common household item, Dr. Smith hung strips of flypaper on the limbs of trees where oropendolas and caciques had built nests. He found that botflies stayed away from the trees that contained the huge nests of wasps and bees. No one knows why. But the flypaper in the trees without bees and wasps collected many botfly bodies.

Having made this discovery, Dr. Smith wondered why some oropendolas and caciques nested in trees *without* bees and wasps. How did those birds protect themselves from botflies?

The answer was surprising. To guard themselves against one parasite—the botfly—oropendolas and caciques accept another parasite, the giant cowbird. And usually, only those oropendolas and caciques that build nests in trees without wasps and bees accept the giant cowbird.

Generally oropendolas and caciques lay no more than two eggs. The giant cowbird deposits only one of her eggs in an oropendola or cacique nest. In a colony of nests built in a tree with bees and wasps, male oropendolas and caciques usually throw cowbird eggs out of their nests in spite of the close resemblance between the cowbird's eggs and their own. But among colonies that build nests in trees without bees and wasps, the female oropendolas and caciques not only accept the foreign eggs in their nests but protect them and allow the cowbird chicks to hatch.

At first this relationship seemed strange to Dr. Smith, but he discovered why it makes sense. Young cowbird chicks hatch five or six days earlier than the chicks of their hosts. When the oropendola and cacique chicks hatch, the young cowbirds remove botfly larvae from their nest-mates. By examining the stomachs of cowbird chicks, Dr. Smith saw that the birds had eaten botfly eggs and larvae, and even mature botflies. Thus more host chicks survive in these nests than in nests that have no protection against botflies. Dr. Smith calls this complex relationship "the advantage of being parasitized." But the story does not end here.

Giant cowbirds have developed elaborate ways of sneaking their eggs into oropendola and cacique nests. Through evolution cowbird eggs have come to mimic the coloring, shape, and size of the eggs laid by various species of oropendolas and caciques. This kind of mimicry seems far removed from that of leaf-shaped insects, but the evolutionary principle is the same in each case. Mimicry is an adaptation that increases the chances of survival of a species.

Of course giant cowbirds prefer laying their eggs in the nests of oropendolas and caciques that will accept them. But Dr. Smith discovered that these cowbirds also find it advantageous to have their eggs accepted in nests constructed near the homes of bees and wasps. (The young of cowbirds, as well as of oropendolas and caciques, are sometimes killed by botflies. Bees and wasps keep away not only these predators but others such as opossums, owls, and toucans.) In the nests of oropendolas and caciques that are near bees and wasps, egg mimicry is especially important, for it sometimes tricks the hosts into accepting eggs they would otherwise throw out.

Because nesting in trees with bees and wasps is so advantageous to oropendola and cacique colonies, Dr. Smith tried to learn why some colonies selected trees without bees and wasps. He found three possible answers. Each involves a hazard which successive generations of these birds, in adapting to their environments, may have learned to avoid. First of all, sometimes wasps and stingless but biting bees desert the tree where they have been nesting. In this case oropendolas and caciques are left without protection. Second, the weight of the birds' nests added to the weight of the wasps' huge nests often causes tree limbs to break, destroying all the nests. Third, bees and wasps construct their nests late in the dry season. If oropendolas and caciques nest in the same tree, they must delay their breeding season. This, too, can be disastrous, because the rainy season may come before young chicks can fly away from their nests. This happened in 1964 and 1967, when the first rains came early and drowned nine colonies with a total loss of 187 chicks.

Dr. Smith does not know exactly how this complex interaction among oropendolas and caciques, wasps and stingless but biting bees, giant cowbirds and botflies evolved. But he has observed it in action. He has documented it and photographed it as a rare example of hosts—in this case oropendolas and caciques—benefiting from a parasite. There may be other equally beneficial host-parasite relationships in tropical forests. This is one of the things that scientists such as Dr. Smith are working to discover.

Bats:
Creatures
of the
Night
World

9

So very little is known about the behavior of tropical bats and how they interact with other forest animals or what role they play in the total ecology of a tropical forest that it is difficult even to classify them. What we do know comes from the work of scientists such as Dr. Charles O. Handley, Jr., of the Smithsonian Institution and Dr. Merlin D. Tuttle of the University of Kansas. Both scientists have studied bats in the New World tropics, and some of Dr. Handley's research was carried out in

(Clockwise, from the bottom)
Two insect-eating bats,
a nectar-eating bat, and
a vampire bat

Panama. Scientists would like to learn more about tropical bats because they are one of the most diverse groups of flying animals in a tropical forest, capable of living in almost every conceivable niche.

Although they have wings and fly, bats are not birds. Like people, monkeys, cows, and pigs, bats are mammals, a group of animals that do not lay eggs but give birth to live young and feed their infants with milk secreted by the female's mammary, or milk-producing, glands. Bats are the only mammals that fly.

Creatures of the night world, bats participate in more food chains than any other group of forest animals. Many species are insectivores (insect eaters), frugivores (fruit eaters), or nectivores (nectar feeders). Some are carnivores, and three species are vampires (blood eaters). Scientists would like to know how such diverse feeding habits evolved.

Equally puzzling, why is it that eighty or more species of tropical bats can coexist in one place while there are seldom as many as ten species living in one place in temperate regions? The area of the Amazon rain forest around Belém, Brazil, has one of the most interesting collections of bats in the world, and bats

Flying fox

in this area have been more thoroughly studied than anyplace else in the New World tropics. Seventy-five species have already been identified. Old World tropical forests also contain bats, although not as many species—but they do have the largest bats in the world, the flying foxes. These fruit-eating bats of the Orient have a wingspread of up to five feet.

Temperate-zone dwellers are familiar with the smaller varieties of bats that sometimes get inside attics in old farmhouses. Hanging upside down during the day, they resemble crumpled masses of gray or brown crepe paper. With their tiny, furry faces and webbed wings, bats seem to be part mouse and part bird.

The expression "blind as a bat" is a joke. Some have good eyesight. Many can see objects as they fly through dark forests, and one species is able to find its way by sighting mountains twenty miles away at night. To locate food in the dark, however, most bats use a nonvisual technique. For a long time this aspect of bat navigation was a mystery, until Dr. Donald R. Griffin of Rockefeller University discovered that bats frequently use a kind of echo-location, or sonar, to find their way.

As a result of many experiments Dr. Griffin learned that both submarine sonar and bat sonar work according to the same principle. A series of vibrations, or waves, move through air or water. When our ears receive the waves, we interpret them as sound. When a wave hits something in its path, an echo is bounced back to the sender. By listening to the echo, a bat or a sonar operator can tell how far away an object is.

As bats fly through the dark forest, they continually send out a series of high-pitched clicks at frequencies far beyond the range of human hearing. The sound waves from these clicks bounce off trees, blossoms, insects—whatever may be in their pathway. In some bats echo-location is so highly developed that they avoid being trapped by the fine strands of nylon mist-nets that scientists use to capture them.

One of the most remarkable known characteristics of bats is the way some species interact with forest vegetation. Certain flowers seem to have evolved features especially designed to attract bats. A large number of bats feed on nectar. Like bees and insects, these bats act as pollinators, helping to transport pollen from blossom to blossom. In the temperate zone most blossoms with which we are familiar close their petals at night. But the bat-pollinated flowers *open* at night, for this is the time that bats search for food. Dull whitish, greenish, or brownish, the flowers are large and tend to have strong, unpleasant odors. In the Malayan rain forest one bat-pollinated tree is called "the midnight horror'' because its flowers open around 10:00 p.m., and by midnight, unlike most flowers which have fragrant scents, they stink.

Vegetation seems also to have evolved along with the fruit-eating bats, whose palates contain ridges against which they crush fruit with their tongues. Some species of vegetarian bats specialize in certain fruits or their juices. Many of these fruits are pendulous (hanging), which makes it easy for bats to locate them as they navigate through the forest at night.

Vampire bats are blood eaters, feeding on large forest birds and other animals, including livestock. Unless they carry rabies, as some do, vampire bats do not kill their prey. But in parts of South and Central America rabid bats are a problem. Foraging in farm areas, these bats sometimes go inside houses and bite people, infecting them with the disease. Unlike vampires in horror movies, however, vampire bats do not transform their victims into fanged monsters thirsting for blood.

Carnivorous rat-eating and lizard-eating bats forage along the forest floor for their food. Fishing bats catch minnows and other small fish for food. These bats live in hollow trees near rivers in the Amazon forest.

Like birds, bats live at all levels of the forest—inside fallen logs, under root ledges along streams, inside hollow trees, and in caves—but so little is known about how bats partition their environment that scientists hesitate to place them in ecological groups. During the day colonies of bats hang motionless from their roosts. Some colonies contain only a dozen or so individuals. Others contain mil-

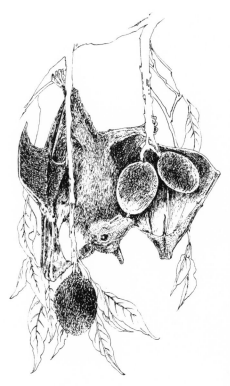

Another fruit-eating bat

lions. When they are roosting, bats usually try to stay out of sight, because it is during this time that they are most likely to be caught by predators.

Studying bats, naturally, involves some night work. Scientists usually set up mist nets or traps about a half hour before sundown. Frequently they work all night capturing bats and recording certain details about each—its age, sex, reproductive condition, molt, and band number (if the bat has been caught previously). Sometimes bats are captured and weighed at regular intervals throughout the night in order to obtain information about the amounts of food consumed and the timing of feeding activities.

Scientists suspect that bats must have a significant impact on the food web, because they are the most massive source of protein in the whole tropical forest system. But much remains to be discovered about the total impact of any species of bat on its environment.

Even less is known about the creatures that prey on bats, although some of their enemies have been identified. In parts of tropical America snakes, particularly boa constrictors, snatch bats from their roosts. Owls and small falcons also prey on bats. One predator, whose diet consists mostly of bats, is known as the bat falcon. In the temperate zone raccoons feed on bats.

There are so many intriguing unanswered questions about tropical bats that one could make a very long list. How did so many diverse species evolve? What kinds of co-evolution have occurred between plants and bats and between bats and other animals? These are only a few of the challenging problems that await future scientists.

Bat falcon

The Monkeys:
Forest
Primates

To people who live in the temperate zone, monkeys are the most familiar animals of the tropical forest, and they are among the most fascinating animals on earth because they are so much like us—or perhaps it would be more fitting to say we are so much like them. Scientists have a special interest in monkeys, particularly in the large apes, because they are our closest relatives in the animal kingdom. In both Old and New World tropics scientists are studying how monkeys communi-

10

cate with each other, how they organize their societies, gather food, and care for their young. People
and monkeys belong to the same biological order
—primates. Our family tree goes back 70 million
years, but, unlike some other primates, we bear little
resemblance to our remote ancestors.

Anthropologists who study the evolution of
human societies have found evidence that man
evolved in tropical Africa. The oldest humanlike, or
humanoid, skull found so far is slightly more than
2 million years old, a fairly recent time in the great
age of the earth. As scientists continue to dig they
may discover another skull, a bone, or a tooth that
will link us with an even more distant past.

Originally, many millions of years ago, primates
lived only in trees and were mostly vegetarians.
Today the great majority of them are still vegetarians,
but they do not all live in trees. As weather, vegetation, and climate changed, some primates descended
to the ground. Accustomed to swinging from tree
to tree, the first primates who tried life on the ground
must have found movement slow and awkward. On
the ground they were exposed to more large predators. But some monkeys adapted to terrestrial life.
Some even ventured outside the forest and developed habits for living on the open grasslands. One
of these adaptations was an upright posture—walking on the hind legs. It is from these primitive,
ground-dwelling, Old World primates who walked
upright and learned to eat meat that we can trace our
own evolution.

Gorillas and chimpanzees, inhabitants of Old
World tropical forests, travel on the ground as well
as in trees. Both species frequently move on their

two hind legs. Largest of the manlike apes, the gorillas wander through forest undergrowth as they forage for the fruit, leaves, and bark that make up their vegetarian diet. The mountain gorilla of the African Congo even eats soil.

New World monkeys can also move about on the ground, but no species spends much time there. In contrast, some Old World monkeys live on the ground.

Other characteristics mark the evolutionary crossroads between Old and New World monkeys, a point many millions of years ago when the two groups began to evolve differently. For example, most New World monkeys have nostrils that are set wide apart. Because of this visible feature, New World monkeys are given the general group name "platyrrhine," which comes from two Greek words: *platys,* meaning "flat," and *rhin,* meaning "nose." In contrast, the nostrils of Old World monkeys are close together, giving them the general name "catarrhine," which means "hook-nosed." We belong to the catarrhine group of primates. New World monkeys play no part in human evolution.

We commonly think of monkeys swinging by their tails, but only New World monkeys have the kind of tail that makes such acrobatics possible. A tail that can grasp branches, vines, or anything else is called "prehensile," which comes from a Latin word meaning "to grasp." The word *comprehension* has the same root, providing a curious link between a monkey's tail and human thought. Not all New World monkeys have prehensile tails, but no Old World monkey has one. In fact, apes do not have tails at all.

(Clockwise, from the bottom)
New World emperor marmoset,
New World night monkey,
Old World chimpanzee,
and Old World rhesus monkey

Old World monkeys are not all tropical. Some live as far north as Tibet, China, and Japan. One of the most wide-ranging species is the macaques. The best-known members of this group are the rhesus monkeys, used for medical and biological experiments and space research.

Apes are the primates most like people. The size and shape of an ape's brain is so similar to ours that the brain of a large ape looks like a miniature human brain. Like us, apes have an appendix and are tailless. Certain details of an ape's skull and skeleton are also humanlike.

In terms of size, no New World monkey comes close to apes and gorillas. Monkeys of tropical America are smaller and spend most of their lives in trees.

Among the apes our closest relatives, chimpanzees, are used for many scientific research projects. Highly intelligent animals, chimpanzees have been taught a variety of skills: building with blocks, uttering a few simple words, smoking a cigar, and pressing levers in a space capsule. The behavior of young chimps and rhesus monkeys is especially instructive to psychologists and animal behaviorists, who find many similarities between these monkeys and apes and young human children.

Another Old World ape that has been studied in detail is the mountain gorilla of the African Congo. This animal lives in groups of about seventeen members, with females outnumbering males as they do in most monkey societies. Even though outnumbered, males dominate the females, and again this is true in many other animal societies, including some human ones.

Mountain gorillas live on the forest floor, where they construct nests each night by bending vegetation toward a center point to make a kind of sleeping platform. Sometimes they also make nests for a midday nap. Because of their size—some old males weigh more than four hundred pounds—mountain gorillas are not bothered by predators. Some gorillas live to be twenty years old, quite a long life span for a tropical forest animal. Life is peaceful among mountain gorillas. Vegetarians, they spend much of their day foraging to satisfy their enormous appetites.

At one time or another you will probably see a Hollywood gorilla beating its hairy chest. Male mountain gorillas do beat their chests but not to frighten people. There are no King Kongs in a tropical forest. Chest beating is the main signal used by

Mountain gorillas

mountain gorillas to communicate over distances. Anyone who has witnessed these animals beating their chests describes it as one of the most impressive sights and sounds in the animal kingdom.

Only the silver-backed males beat their chests. The display begins with a series of hoots. Then the gorilla beats his chest with both hands. Because of the sacs in his chest that are inflated with air, a drumlike sound travels through the forest. After beating his chest the gorilla runs wildly from side to side, hitting at branches. He finishes by hitting the ground with the palm of his hand. Chest beating occurs when two silver-backed mountain gorillas see each other over a distance. These displays seem to function both as threats and as announcements of territorial claim.

On Barro Colorado Island there are five species of primates typical of New World tropical forests: marmosets, howler monkeys, spider monkeys, cebus monkeys, and night monkeys. For these primates who are entirely arboreal the branches and lianas are highways through the forest. New World primates use their highways in various ways. Howler monkeys travel on top of the branches. Spider monkeys often travel underneath them and swing from tree to tree.

In the canopy monkeys fill a niche similar to that of army ants on the forest floor. As monkeys move through the trees they stir up insects, which are eaten by birds. Of the five primate species living on Barro Colorado all except the night monkeys forage during the day. These nocturnal primates are unique among monkeys, who are usually daytime creatures.

Most monkeys communicate with visual signals, but the night monkey does not. In the deep blackness of a forest night visual signals would be useless. Like other nocturnal creatures, the night monkey communicates with sounds. During the day this monkey sleeps in a hole in a tree until the sun disappears. Then it forages for insects, eggs, and small birds.

Marmosets are the smallest and most primitive monkeys. Canopy dwellers, marmosets feed mostly on insects, but they also eat fruit, seeds, and plant shoots. Some marmosets have striking faces and coloration. One, the lion marmoset, gets its name from the shaggy red mane that fringes its face.

The trapeze artists of New World tropical forests are the spider monkeys. Using their long forelimbs, spider monkeys swing nimbly from branch to branch, a type of movement called "brachiation." Their prehensile tail is tipped with a small patch of ridged skin which acts as a nonskid tire, enabling a spider monkey to use its tail as an additional hand to grip branches or fruit. While feeding, spider monkeys often use their tails to anchor themselves to a limb.

Canopy fruits are the chief food on the spider monkey's menu. Messy eaters, these monkeys munch on their food and drop half-eaten fruits to the forest floor. But fruit dropping is important in tropical forest ecology because it provides a source of food for forest-floor animals. Fruit dropping also aids the vegetation, providing a way for seeds to reach the ground, where they can eventually sprout.

Spider monkeys playfully roam from the lower to the upper canopy and frequently descend to the

Spider monkeys

ground. They, too, travel in groups in which females outnumber males. Babies ride on their mother's back by clinging to her long hair.

On Barro Colorado spider monkeys have grown accustomed to being stared at by human primates. Occasionally they stare back and even come close enough to feed from your hand.

Spider monkeys sometimes socialize with another species of New World primates, the small, white-faced cebus capucines. This species is named after the Roman Catholic order of Capucine monks because the tuft of black hair on top of a cebus monkey's head resembles a monk's hood.

Dr. John Oppenheimer of Johns Hopkins University spent several summers studying cebus monkeys on Barro Colorado. He paid close attention to their feeding habits, which play a significant role in the forest's ecology.

Foraging in groups throughout various levels of the forest, cebus monkeys eat different kinds of flowers, buds, ticks, spiders, walking sticks, grasshoppers, termites, and other insects. Such a diet helps to keep the forest's insect population under control.

Moisture in fruits and rainwater in holes supply the cebus monkey's needs for liquid.

When threatened by predators or intruders, cebus monkeys break off branches and drop them to the forest floor. Although these flying missiles sometimes land on the heads of curious scientists, stick breaking helps forest vegetation. As efficiently as gardeners with pruning shears, cebus monkeys usually select dead branches that the tree no longer needs.

Dr. Oppenheimer discovered an even more intimate relationship between cebus monkeys and the vegetation. A favorite food of these monkeys are the terminal buds of the gustavia tree, which is in the Brazil nut family. Terminal buds grow on the ends of branches. By feeding on these buds, cebus monkeys affect the tree's growth. Compared with gustavia trees on Panama's mainland, where there are no cebus monkeys, the gustavia trees on Barro Colorado show greater branching. Increased branching enables a tree to produce more buds, which in turn produce fruits and seeds. By feeding on terminal buds, cebus monkeys actually increase their future food supply.

Cebus monkeys

Other monkeys also interact with forest vegetation.

Fruits and leaves make up the diet of howler
monkeys, who live in the upper canopy. Unlike
spider monkeys, howlers tend to eat all of a fruit—
skin, pulp, and seeds. Some seeds will not sprout
unless they have been eaten by a howler and have
passed through the monkey's digestive tract.

You can tell when howlers are ready to begin

foraging. Just before dawn the forest stillness is suddenly broken by roars that can be heard for several miles. As howler groups awaken, the male monkeys who dominate each group roar for several minutes.

Using a powerful, thick, bony vessel in his throat, a male howler can outroar any lion or bull. Air forced into the throat vessel expands as the howler makes a sound which gives him the distinction of being the loudest New World primate. Indians named the howler "Caraya," which means "chief of the woods." In his studies of these monkeys, Dr. C. R. Carpenter of Pennsylvania State University has observed that the male howler uses his roar as a signal in at least three ways.

In the morning each dominant male roars to direct his group's feeding. As the male leader moves through the treetops, his roar signals the other members of his group to follow.

Howlers also roar to frighten intruders. In this case the bark is much more terrifying than the bite, for howlers are peaceful animals and rarely fight.

When two male howlers from two different groups meet each other, they begin to roar. In this case each male uses his roar to claim a particular territory for his own group. The roaring duel continues until one group backs off and leaves.

Moving on all fours, howlers crawl along the tops of branches as they forage. Traveling together, a group may range over two hundred yards in a day. In contrast to the agile spider monkeys, howlers move slowly. Largest of the New World monkeys, howlers spend most of their time eating and sleeping in the canopy. They come to the forest floor only to rescue a fallen infant.

On Barro Colorado howlers have no predators except for boa constrictors, who occasionally eat one of their babies. Yet there is no population explosion among howlers on the island, for yellow fever and parasitic botflies help to limit their numbers.

Howlers, like other monkeys, communicate not only with sound but also with their other senses —sight, touch, and smell. Unlike people, who use a spoken language to send most of their messages, other animals rely more on their other senses to communicate.

We are most familiar with sound as a means of communication because we speak words every day, but we also use visual signals to communicate. The wink of an eye, the signal of a green traffic light, the wave of an umpire's arm, a baseball player's tugging his cap all communicate messages without speaking one word. Body language or other non-verbal language can sometimes communicate more forcefully than words.

Almost all species of monkeys that live in social groups communicate with touch in the form of grooming, or cleaning each other. Just as a mother cat cleans, or grooms, her kitten by licking its fur, so mother monkeys groom their infants by picking insects out of their fur. Adult monkeys, males and females, also groom each other. The close physical contact through grooming helps to keep peace within a group of monkeys at the same time that it removes parasites from their backs.

In his studies of the titi monkeys of South America Dr. Martin Moynihan observed touch used in a different way. Seated side by side, two titi monkeys intertwine their long, bushy tails into a thick cable. Both grooming and tail twining are social activities that help to maintain friendly relationships within a group.

Most monkeys communicate with a variety of facial expressions when they are within close enough range. When approached by an intruder cebus monkeys open their mouths in a wide, toothy grimace. This threat display is accompanied by high-pitched sounds. Mountain gorillas confront intruders with a full-face glare. Female mountain gorillas signal submission by looking away. Chimpanzees communicate with a great variety of sounds and facial expressions.

Branch shaking is an aggressive display among gorillas, red spider monkeys, chimpanzees, and rhesus monkeys.

Monkeys use visual signals only when they are close enough together to see each other. Howlers, who live in the dense foliage of the upper canopy, have few visual signals, but a roar does not have to be seen in order to be understood.

Squirrel monkeys communicate in such an elaborate pattern of birdlike sounds that one scientist has actually made a dictionary of squirrel-monkey language. By studying the development of sounds in monkeys, scientists such as Dr. Martin Moynihan and Dr. Peter Marler may learn more about the evolution of human speech.

Body odor is another means of communication used by many animals. Ants mark trails with odors. Dogs mark a favorite fire hydrant or tree by urinating on it. Human males and females use scents to attract members of the opposite sex—but not their natural body odors. People do all they can to disguise their body odors with the synthetic chemical odors of perfumes, mouthwashes, and deodorants.

Some monkeys mark territory by sliding their backsides along branches. Special scent glands leave an odor that becomes a calling card and an invitation for other monkeys of the same species.

A male titi monkey's scent glands are located in the center of his chest. By lowering his chest and rubbing it along a branch, a male titi leaves his mark. Scent is also important when two titis greet each other. When introduced for the first time inside a laboratory cage, two titis sniff each other.

Chimpanzees not only communicate with each other in a variety of ways but also respond to the alarm calls of birds and other animals. Being alert to danger when it is signaled by other species gives chimpanzees an additional survival advantage, one that would be equivalent to our knowing the word for "danger" in another language.

Monkeys have fascinated people for a long time. We have an old saying, "Monkey see, monkey do," to describe how children imitate adults, a learning process that also occurs among chimpanzees and other apes.

We share with other primates a tropical past, yet we have learned to survive in every corner of the planet while they still live in tropical forests much as their ancestors did millions of years ago.

How did we get out of these forests? What has made us the way we are today?

As scientists continue to study tropical forest primates, we may learn the answers to these questions. We may also learn whether our life span as a species will extend as far into the future as the family trees of other species reach back into the past.

Science
and
Tropical
Forests

Scientists believe that tropical forests hold many secrets that can benefit man if only he is given enough time to discover them. Thousands of acres of tropical forest have already been destroyed for plantation agriculture—rubber, coffee, and cocoa. Each year more bulldozers move into the forests to cut lumber and to build highways. The 3,000-mile Trans-Amazon Highway, now being constructed in Brazil, is only the first section of a

11

giant 9,000-mile network of roads that may crisscross the Amazon River Basin. Well-constructed highways are necessary to the economic development of any country, but the Trans-Amazon Highway raises some serious questions. Many scientists consider it an enormous threat to the largest tropical forest left on earth.

For the thousands of people who will build homes along this highway, thousands of forest animals will be displaced, their habitats destroyed. Plant and animal species, including some tribes of forest Indians, will begin dying out. For the new homesteaders, the extra land may seem like an immediate benefit. But is it in the long run? As we have seen, the poor tropical soil will not support agriculture beyond two or three seasons. How will the people earn their livelihoods when the soil will no longer yield crops? At the present rate of destruction, the entire Amazon rain forest may be leveled within thirty-five years. Thousands of rare plant and animal species found nowhere else on earth will disappear forever. Worst of all, man will have bolted a door to discovery, cutting off all chance of learning what this vast forest ecosystem might have to offer present and future generations. Such destruction would truly be a crime against nature.

No one knows what consequences our planet would suffer if tropical forests disappeared. Scientists do know that we all live on one biosphere—the earth with its atmosphere and oceans. Whatever happens in one part of our biosphere affects the population of the entire world. The English poet John Donne wrote: "No man is an island, entire of itself; every man is a piece of the continent, a part of the main." This seventeenth-century poet stated an ecological truth. Just as life in a tropical forest is linked by subtle interrelationships, so is all life on earth.

Concentrated in tropical forests are many serious ecological problems also found in areas outside these forests—food shortages, erosion, overpopulation, and disease. But a tropical forest is neither threatened nor destroyed by these problems. Somehow they are solved within the web of dynamic interactions among plants and animals that makes the forest self-perpetuating. By studying tropical forests, scientists hope to learn more about the laws of competition that enable such a diverse community to remain so stable.

Some scientists believe that in tropical forests man can find cures for most viral diseases, if only there is time to discover these cures. They wonder why, for example, some tropical forest animals are immune to viruses that cause diseases in other kinds of animals outside the forest.

Hoping to answer this challenging question, scientists established a virus research laboratory in 1954 in Belém, Brazil. By collecting animals and testing their blood, an international team of investigators is trying to understand viruses by learning as much as possible about the animals that carry them.

One virus under study causes a disease known as St. Louis encephalitis, an inflammation of the brain that causes muscle weakness and drowsiness and is sometimes fatal to people. Belém, Brazil, is a long way from St. Louis, Missouri, but the virus turns up in both places. American doctors believe that migrating birds carry the virus without being affected by it themselves.

At the virus research laboratory scientists discovered that the route of the encephalitis virus from birds to people involves an intermediary—the mosquito. Mosquitoes get the virus by biting birds. And mosquitoes bite people. When a mosquito carrying the St. Louis encephalitis virus bites a person, that person becomes infected with the disease. When someone discovers why the birds carrying the virus do not become ill, doctors may learn how to protect people against the disease.

Throughout the world's tropical areas mosquitoes carry not only the encephalitis viruses but also the virus that causes yellow fever. Another virus-caused disease is rabies, carried in the tropics by the vampire bat. Too small to be seen with anything other than an electron microscope, viruses cause many well-known diseases, including measles.

Another group of diseases is caused by microscopic animals, flagellated protozoans, that live as parasites in the tissues of various blood-sucking insects and in mammals. The "kissing bug" carries one of these, Chagas' disease, to man.

Like other forms of life, parasites and viruses flourish in the tropics, making them rich areas for medical research. Many viruses have been discovered in the Amazon forest, and new ones will probably continue to be found. But the great mystery is the tropical forest's resistance to many of the viruses it houses. Some kind of immunity seems built into a tropical forest's ecology.

Crowded into cities, people are subject to epidemics. In tropical forests monkey populations are susceptible to yellow fever, another disease whose virus is carried by mosquitoes. Yet the forest teems with all kinds of living things and there are no vast

"Kissing bug"

epidemics such as those that have swept through human populations. It is possible that what seems to be immunity within the forest involves happy host-parasite relations such as that between oropendolas and caciques and the giant cowbird. The entire subject of forest immunity offers a rich frontier for scientific research. If scientists can learn why this immunity exists, they may also discover how to cure most of our virus diseases.

Brazil's Ministry of Agriculture has already benefited from a discovery made at the research station in Belém. Inside the rain forest at Belém there is a fungus-resistant pepper. In the agricultural area outside the forest peppers are an important crop raised for export. But in recent years the pepper crop was destroyed by the same fungus that has no effect on the rain-forest pepper.

A Brazilian scientist decided to conduct an experiment. He grafted the top of a field-grown pepper onto the bottom of a rain-forest pepper. The result was a fungus-resistant pepper that could be cultivated outside the forest.

Forest Indians seem as resistant to tropical viruses as the plants and animals. But these same Indians are susceptible to our childhood diseases such as whooping cough and measles. African pygmies even get sunstroke outside the rain forest.

At the Mabali Research Station on Lake Tumba in Africa, scientists are studying tribes like the pygmies who spend their lives in the forest, far from cities, automobiles, television sets, and airplanes. By the living standards of temperate-zone dwellers, forest tribes are primitive, cut off from what we call civilization. But these Stone Age tribes may have something to teach us about survival. They have learned to live at peace with nature. The Tasadays of Mindanao in the Philippines have no word in their vocabulary for war. We compete with the rest of nature, trying to harness it for our own, often destructive purposes. Forest tribes take only what they need from their environment. We have taken over most of the ecological niches on our planet, slowly crowding out other species. Forest tribes share their environment with other species. While we have assaulted our environment, primitive tribes have been living as *part of* the forest rather than *apart from* it.

Of course, we cannot abandon our own life styles and wander back into the forests. Science and technology alone have not polluted our air or our water or destroyed our forests. It is the way we have used our inventions which has done the damage. Thinking ecologically involves long-range planning; it requires us to consider thoughtfully what will happen not just ten years in the future but centuries ahead. We can use our technology creatively, to work *with* nature instead of *against* it—to renew the resources of our planet instead of exhausting them.

Like a tropical forest system, our entire planet Earth is an enormously diverse ecosystem. The future survival of this planet will depend on maintaining balanced relationships among its plants, its waters, its atmosphere, and its various inhabitants.

At the Smithsonian Tropical Research Institute scientists are particularly interested in the relationship between survival and diversity. As a vast natural system, a tropical forest has a long history of survival, as we have seen. In spite of its enormous diversity a tropical forest is a stable, self-contained system. Scientists believe that the coexistence of thousands of different plant and animal species is a clue to the forest's long survival. Perhaps variety is as necessary to life as food, water, and air.

Tropical forests may be necessary for the survival of our planet. So far they have played an important role in the evolution of species. It was in tropical forests that most land plants and animals, including man, evolved. A tropical forest is where we began—our cradle of life.

Scientists say that tropical forests are evolutionary reservoirs—places where conditions favor evolution twenty-four hours a day. Just as a water reservoir acts as a storage tank for a community's liquid needs, so tropical forests are a kind of storage tank for the evolutionary needs of our entire planet. These needs are not so obvious as thirst. Evolution is a slow process occurring over many millions of years. We cannot see evolution taking place, but we can observe its results. Without evolution, whales would still be flopping around on land in the shape of their cowlike ancestors. Most land creatures might still have fins and gills. Without a place to improve and change, man might never have gotten out of the trees. Without a place for new plants and animals to develop, species might eventually reach a dead end and, like the dinosaurs, become extinct.

The rate at which tropical forests are being destroyed raises some hard questions:

What will happen to the soil that is now protected by tropical forests in hilly regions? Without vegetation to hold moisture, would the rain wash away the soil, eventually turning these areas into deserts?

What will we substitute for the raw materials

such as timber, fuel, resins, and gums that now come from tropical forests?

Can our atmosphere afford to lose the oxygen produced by tropical forest vegetation?

What will happen to world weather patterns if tropical forests disappear?

Can man afford to destroy the place where he and thousands of other creatures evolved?

Can we afford to lose forests that can never be replaced, forests that hold clues to our past and that may contain the keys to our future survival?

At the moment there are no answers, only a hope that scientists will be given time to search in the few places on earth where answers might be found—tropical forests.

For Further Reading

Bates, Henry Walter. *The Naturalist on the River Amazons.* Berkeley: University of California Press, 1962.

Bates, Marston, and the Editors of Life. *The Land and Wildlife of South America* (a volume in the *Life* Nature Library). New York: Time, Inc., 1964.

Carpenter, C. R. *Naturalistic Behavior of Nonhuman Primates.* University Park, Pa: The Pennsylvania State University Press, 1964.

Carr, Archie, and the Editors of Life. *The Land and Wildlife of Africa* (a volume in the *Life* Nature Library). New York: Time, Inc., 1964.

Carrington, Richard, and the Editors of Life. *The Mammals* (a volume in the *Life* Nature Library. A Young Readers edition is also available). New York: Time, Inc., 1963.

De La Rue, Edgar Aubert; Bourliere, Francois; Harroy, Jean-Paul. *The Tropics.* New York: Alfred A. Knopf, 1957.

Dorst, Jean. *South America and Central America.* New York: Random House, 1967.

Eimerl, Sarel; DeVore, Irven; and the Editors of Life. *The Primates* (a volume in the *Life* Nature Library. A Young Readers edition is also available). New York: Time, Inc., 1965.

Farb, Peter, and the Editors of Life. *The Forest* (a volume in the *Life* Nature Library). New York: Time, Inc., 1961.

Fascinating World of Animals. Readers Digest Books (New York: W. W. Norton), 1971.

MacLeish, Kenneth. "Stone-Age Cavemen of Mindanao." *National Geographic,* Aug. 1972, pp. 219–248.

Richards, Paul W. *The Life of the Jungle.* New York: McGraw-Hill, 1970.

——— . *The Tropical Rain Forest, an Ecological Study.* New York: Cambridge University Press, 1957.

Ripley, S. Dillon, and the Editors of Life. *The Land and Wildlife of Tropical Asia* (a volume in the *Life* Nature Library). New York: Time, Inc., 1964.

Schaller, George B. *The Mountain Gorilla.* Chicago: University of Chicago Press, 1963.

Index

ABOUT THE AUTHOR

Mary Batten was born and raised in Smithfield, Virginia. She attended the University of North Carolina in Greensboro and was graduated from the New School for Social Research in New York City. At the New School she won the Goldman Award for the best essay of the year on American literature and later a Fulbright fellowship to study in France. She received an M.A. degree from the Columbia University School of Graduate Studies.

Until she visited the Smithsonian Institution's tropical research station on Barro Colorado Island in Panama, Ms. Batten believed, like many other people, that tropical forests were frightening places, filled with terrifying creatures. As part of her research for a film she was working on, she followed scientists around the island, sliding down gullies to reach a colony of leaf-cutting ants, traveling by boat to a tiny island where iguanas nest, even going out at night to observe the forest. She says, "The real forest is much more exciting than anything we have been taught to believe about 'jungles.'"

Ms. Batten is the author of another book for young people, *Discovery by chance: Science and the Unexpected.* She lives in New York City.

ABOUT THE ILLUSTRATOR

Betty Fraser was born in Massachusetts and graduated from the Rhode Island School of Design. She has illustrated many books for children. Miss Fraser now lives in New York City.